# DURHAM
# MILLENNIUM

*A Thousand Years of Durham City*

*by*

## DAVID SIMPSON

Sponsored by

**MILLBURNGATE**
SHOPPING CENTRE

## DURHAM CITY

# Introduction

One thousand years ago in the late summer of 995 AD Durham entered the history books for the first time when a group of wandering monks, carrying with them the coffin of St. Cuthbert settled on the naturally defended site then called Dun Holm. Here they established the final resting place for their saint and a church was built to house the saint's remains. Gradually a city developed around this site which became one of England's greatest centres of Christian pilgrimage. Later in 1093 a great Norman cathedral was built which is still regarded as one of the finest examples of church architecture in Europe. Since that time Durham has seen many changes and a number of modern developments, but it is still essentially a small city, with extensive open spaces and numerous wooded river banks.

This book explores the City of Durham and its surrounding villages and has two major features - a guide to the colourful characters, places and buildings of the city's past and a unique chronicle of all the major events and happenings in the city's history from 995 to the present day. The chronicle which runs throughout the book takes the form of newspaper headlines most of which The Northern Echo was not around to report before its foundation in 1870. I hope you will find this book of interest and share with me my great love for this city of one thousand years.

David Simpson August 1995

**Acknowledgments**

Thanks to Publications Editor Sue Kendrew, to Colin Hagan for designing the book, to Iain Watson of Durham County Libraries, and to all the staff of Durham City Reference Library for their help over the years. Thanks also to The Media Factory, Denise, Debbie, Elli and Joyce for their hard work behind the scenes. Special thanks to MILLBURNGATE SHOPPING CENTRE

# Contents

# Origins of the City

## June 8th 793
### VIKINGS RAID ISLAND
**Lindisfarne**

*In an unprecedented attack which has shocked the whole of Europe, an army of Vikings from Norway raided Lindisfarne today. Monks fled in fear and many were slaughtered, Bishop Higbald has sought refuge on the mainland. The Vikings are attracted by the huge wealth of the Lindisfarne monastery which is a great centre of pilgrimage. Pilgrims visiting the holy shrine of St Cuthbert have bestowed many gifts to the monastery making it a source of rich picking for the Vikings.*

## June 8th 793
### SLAUGHTER
**Lindisfarne**

*An Anglo-Saxon Chronicler has made a written record of the terrible Viking raid on Lindisfarne. His account is as follows; '793. In this year terrible portents appeared over Northumbria, which sorely affrighted the inhabitants: there were exceptional flashes of lightning, and fiery dragons were seen flying through the air. A great famine followed hard upon these signs; and a little later in that same year, on the 8th June, the harrying of the heathen miserably destroyed God's church by rapine and slaughter.*

## ST CUTHBERT, LINDISFARNE & THE VIKINGS

The story of Durham begins with St Cuthbert, a seventh century Northumbrian saint who at the age of seventeen entered the monastery of Melrose near the River Tweed to become a monk. His outstanding qualities - a fair and placid manner, a remarkable talent for athletics and a reputed gift for working miracles are certain to have attracted attention and not surprisingly Cuthbert quickly gained promotion. Ultimately he was appointed to the post of bishop on the island of Lindisfarne just off the Northumberland coast.

As a bishop Cuthbert travelled widely throughout the north and played an important part in encouraging people to follow the Christian faith which had only recently been introduced to Northumbria.

Later in his life Cuthbert retired from the post of bishop to pursue life as a hermit on the remote island of Inner Farne, one of a group of small islands to the south east of Lindisfarne. Here Cuthbert was visited by many pilgrims but for most of the time he was occupied by prayer having only the sea birds and seals for company. It was here on Inner Farne in the year 687 A.D that Cuthbert finally died in the fifty second year of his life.

In accordance with an agreement made by Cuthbert during his life, his body was removed from Inner Farne and taken to Lindisfarne for burial. There it remained for a number of years until the monks decided to remove the coffin for inspection. On removal of the body, the monks were astonished to find the corpse in a totally incorrupt state - it had not decayed. This remarkable discovery was seen as a miracle and Cuthbert was proclaimed a saint.

When the news of the miracle spread, huge numbers of pilgrims travelled from far and wide to visit Lindisfarne. This made the monastery on the island extremely wealthy from gifts bestowed by the visitors who were in effect the tourists of their time, indeed it is possible to speculate that St Cuthbert's body had been embalmed and that the miracle had been proclaimed with the sole intention of encouraging 'tourists' to visit the island.

*Lindisfarne Castle, Holy Island*

If this was the case, we cannot be too critical of the monks for wishing to sustain their livelihood through 'tourism' on the death of their saint. Sadly, the increasing wealth of the Lindisfarne monastery ultimately attracted visitors of a most unwelcome kind in the form of the Vikings who came to raid and plunder the island for its riches in 793 A.D.

But what, you may ask, has this got to do with the origins of Durham City? Well the answer is this - as the Viking raids on Lindisfarne continued throughout the following century, the monks of the Holy Island were forced to flee to the mainland. They took with them the coffin of St Cuthbert and other valuable relics like the famous Lindisfarne Gospels.

> *How when the rude Dane burn'd their pile,*
> *The monks fled forth from Holy Isle,*
> *O'er northern mountain, marsh and moor,*
> *From sea to sea, from shore to shore,*
> *Seven years Saint Cuthbert's corpse they bore.*
>
> Sir Walter Scott

For many years the monks and their successors carried the coffin around the north of England , settling for a time at Norham on Tweed, at Chester le Street and at Ripon before settling at Durham in the year 995 AD. The story behind their settlement at Durham is related in the legend of the Dun Cow

# 995 - IN THE BEGINNING

*A detail from St. Cuthbert's coffin*

In 995 A.D after years of wandering the north, the carriers of St Cuthbert's coffin came to a halt at a hill called Warden Law, the site of an Iron Age fort near Hetton to the east of Durham. Here the vehicle on which the coffin was transported came to stand still and despite the efforts of the whole congregation of followers who tried to push, the coffin would not move.

Aldhun, Bishop of Chester le Street, the leader of the congregation, committed the monks to three days of fasting and prayer in order to learn the reason why the coffin would not move. After a period of intense meditation their prayers were finally answered when St Cuthbert appeared in a vision to a monk called Eadmer. St Cuthbert instructed Eadmer that the coffin should be taken to a place called Dun Holm.

The monks had not heard of Dun Holm, but may have been aware that its name meant 'Hill Island'. Dun was an Anglo-Saxon word meaning `hill', Holm meaning 'island' is a word of Scandinavian origin. Dun Holm was later called Duresme by the Normans and was known in Latin as Dunelm. Over the years the name has been simplified to the modern form -Durham.

## 793
### SCHOLAR ATTACKS MORAL STANDARDS
**France**

*In a letter sent from the Carolignian court in Europe, Alcuin the great scholar of York has blamed the recent Viking attack on a fall in moral standards by the leaders of Northumbria. The Viking raid may be seen as punishment from God, but others may say that the weakness and instability caused by constant civil war in the Northumbrian kingdom makes it vulnerable to external attack.*

## 883
### DANES GRANT CHESTER-LE-STREET TO CUTHBERT FOLK
**Chester-le-Street**

*Guthred the Dane, the new Danish King of York, has granted an area of land between the Rivers Tyne and Tees to the community of St Cuthbert, who have recently fled from the island of Lindisfarne after continuous Viking raids. The grant of this land signifies the beginning of what will later become County Durham. The Community of St Cuthbert has settled within this territory at Chester-le-Street (Conecaster). St Cuthbert's body was interred in a new church here and Eardwulf, the former Bishop of Lindisfarne, has become the first Bishop of Chester-le-Street.*

## 952
### ERIC BLOODAXE VISITS CHESTER-LE-STREET
**Chester-le-Street**

*Eric Bloodaxe, the Viking King of York, has visited the shrine of St Cuthbert at Chester-le-Street. His action of pilgrimage has become something of a tradition among powerful kings. In previous years visitors to St Cuthbert's shrine at Chester-le-Street have included Kings Athelstan, Edmund and Eadred.*

## 990
### ALDHUN NEW BISHOP
**Chester-le-Street**

*Aldhun has become the Bishop of Chester-le-Street. He will be the last person to hold this post.*

*Late Summer 995*

**CITY OF DURHAM FOUNDED BY MONKS**

*After a short stay at Ripon the monks of St Cuthbert's community who recently fled from Chester-le-Street with the body of St Cuthbert have returned north to settle at a naturally defended site called Dunholm (Durham). The site is almost like a wooded island, formed by the horse-shoe shaped gorge of the River Wear.*

*995*

**EARLY MINSTER BUILT**

*A wooden minster called the White Church has been constructed for St Cuthbert's remains at Durham. Uchtred Eadulfson of Bamburgh employed labour from the River Coquet in Northumberland to the River Tees to fortify the site and Aldhun, who was formerly the Bishop of Chester-le-Street, has become the first Bishop of Durham.*

*999*

**STONE MINSTER BUILT**

*A new minster called the White Church, a small Anglo Saxon cathedral of stone, has been constructed at Durham for the shrine of St Cuthbert. It replaces an earlier White Church built in 995.*

*1003*

**DARLINGTON GIVEN TO BISHOP OF DURHAM**
**York**

*Darlington has been given to the Bishop of Durham by Styr the son of Ulphus at a ceremony in York. Archbishop Wulfstan and King Athelred were present. Darlington may have been part of the territory seized by the Irish-Norse king Ragnald in 918.*

*1006*

**SCOTS MASSACRED**

*The Scots under the leadership of King Malcolm were heavily defeated by North Easterners during an attack on Durham City. King Malcolm was attempting to seize the North-East, which a succession of Scottish kings have claimed as their own. Heads of the best looking Scottish soldiers were displayed around the city walls following the battle and some Durham women were presented with the generous gift of a cow for washing the*

# LEGEND OF THE DUN COW

On learning the name of their destination the monks found that they were now able to move the coffin. Proceeding west through some well wooded countryside they asked a number of local people where they could find the Dun Holm but unfortunately no-one had heard of such a place. Luckily by chance in an area later known as Mount Joy a milkmaid was overheard asking another milkmaid if she had seen her Dun Cow, a grey coloured beast that had wandered off on its own. The other maid answered that she had seen the cow roaming about near Dun Holm.

When the monks heard mention of Dun Holm they were filled with joy - hence Mount Joy, and followed the footsteps of the milk maid as she searched for her cow. By this stroke of luck or Divine Providence, they were able to find the site of Dunholm - a wooded 'Hill - Island' peninsula formed by a tight gorge-like meander of the River Wear. The legend of how Durham was first discovered is remembered in an eighteenth century carving on the north wall of Durham Cathedral, which depicts the milk maid and her Dun Cow. Sadly the story of the Dun Cow seems to be little more than a legend and can be traced to no earlier than the eighteenth century - the date of the carving.

# THE WHITE CHURCH

Dun Holm provided an ideally defended site for the resting place of St Cuthbert. It was on high ground protected on three sides by the steep wooded gorge of the River Wear. Firstly however the site had to be cleared of its thick woodland and the wood provided ideal building material for the first houses in the newly born City of Durham.

A small, temporary church was built from the boughs of the trees to house St Cuthbert's coffin and this building is said to have occupied the site of the present church of St Mary le Bow. The 'church of boughs' was replaced a few days later by a white-washed wooden building called The White Church or Alba Ecclesia built in the centre of the Dun Holm peninsula. The White Church remained in use until September 4th 998 A.D when it was replaced by a second `White Church', an Anglo-Saxon minster, built of stone.

The people who constructed the new minster came from all parts of Northumbria from the Coquet to the River Tees and were employed by Uchtred, a powerful Anglo-Saxon earl who ruled the whole region. The minster was presided over by the Bishop called Aldhun who was Uchtred's Father-in-Law. Aldhun was the first Bishop of Durham but had previously been the Bishop of nearby Chester le Street where he was still an important landowner.

# KEEPING THE SCOTS OUT

The ancient area called Northumbria included Durham and was a troublesome region that withstood many invasions. The Vikings for example had captured lands in southern Northumbria to form the great Viking kingdom centred upon York which occupied the whole Yorkshire area.

By the time the monks had settled at Durham the Vikings were not so great an enemy as the Scots who were to pose a threat to the wealthy shrine of St Cuthbert at Durham for many years to come. Durham's defensive position was clearly going to be of importance.

The advantages of Durham's defensive position were fully realised in 1006 when the Scots made their first attack on the small city. Fortunately the Scots were quickly repelled and many of the invaders lost their heads to an army of English comprised of Northumbrians and Yorkshiremen. The captured Scottish heads were displayed around the Durham City walls as a menacing warning against further attack. Four of the city's women were each presented with the generous gift of a cow for washing the heads and combing the hair of the best looking Scots which were displayed around the city.

## A PLACE OF PILGRIMAGE

As well as being an important defensive site Durham was also an important place of pilgrimage. The early cathedral and shrine at Durham were visited by hundreds of pilgrims who came to visit Durham in the same way as the pilgrims who had visited Lindisfarne a century before. Among the visitors to Durham was King Canute the Dane (1017 1035), who as a mark of respect, walked six miles bare footed to the site from Garmondsway, which is now a deserted medieval village situated near Coxhoe.

As a gift King Canute returned some of the land that had been taken from the Bishops of Durham by his Viking ancestors. The land included the large estate owned by King Canute in the Tees valley, centred upon Staindrop and Gainford, near Darlington.

## THE CONQUEROR'S VISIT

When the Normans invaded Britain in 1066 under William the Conqueror they may have been aware of the fatal defeat of the Scots at Durham years before, but were not deterred in their aim to take control of the city. In fact William the Conqueror is said to have visited Durham with the intention of viewing the incorrupted body of St Cuthbert.

William ordered his men to expose St Cuthbert's body from its tomb and warned that he would put to death all Durham churchmen of senior rank if it were found that the saint's body was not in an incorrupt state. Mysteriously before the king had even looked at the saint's coffin he found himself breathless and panic stricken by a sudden burning fever.

Thinking himself to be possessed by some strange force associated with Saint Cuthbert he quickly fled from Durham and would not dismount his horse until he had crossed the River Tees into Yorkshire which was seemingly outside the limits of St Cuthbert's mysterious powers.

The lane by which the king made his hasty retreat from Durham acquired the name of 'King's Ride' or Kingsgate. In those days the lane led to a ford across the River Wear. Today it is called Bow Lane and leads across the River Wear by means of the Kingsgate Footbridge.

heads and combing their hair. The men who defeated the Scots were led by Uchtred son of the elderly Earl of Bamburgh. Uchtred is also the son-in-law of the Bishop of Durham.

### 1016
#### BISHOP DIES
Aldhun the first Bishop of Durham has died. He was said to have been heartbroken by the news of the defeat of the Northumbrians at the Battle of Carham on Tweed and the loss of his north Northumbrian lands.

### 1022
#### BEDE'S BONES PINCHED
**Jarrow**
The relics of the Venerable Bede have been brought to Durham from Jarrow by Aelfred the Durham sacrist and relic collector. Aelfred is a notorious collector of saint's relics which he 'acquires' from ruined monasteries in the north.

### 1027
#### KING VISITS DURHAM
Following his recent pilgrimage to Rome, King Canute has visited Durham where he walked bare foot from Garmondsway, six miles south of the city, to visit the shrine of St Cuthbert. Canute has bestowed certain lands (in County Durham) to the community of St Cuthbert at Durham. The lands may be territories seized by the Norse king Ragnald in 918.

### 1038
#### SCOTS REPELLED
King Duncan of Scotland has besieged Durham City but the attack has been repelled. Duncan was heavily defeated and has fled to Scotland. The attack on Durham is linked with the Scottish desire to make North Eastern England a part of Scotland.

### 1056
#### LAST SAXON BISHOP
Aegelwine has become the Bishop of Durham following the resignation of Bishop Athelric. Aegelwine will be the last Anglo-Saxon to hold the Durham bishopric post.

## Oct 14th 1066

### BATTLE OF HASTINGS
**Sussex**

*William of Normandy has defeated the Anglo-Saxon King of England, Harold Godwinson in battle at Hastings today. Harold, who recently defeated the Norwegian King Harald Hardrad in battle at York, was killed, reputedly by an arrow in the eye. William known as 'the Conqueror' will become the new King of England.*

## January 30th 1069

### NORMANS SEIZE CITY
*Robert de Comine the newly appointed Norman Earl of Northumbria and his Norman army of seven hundred men have seized control of the City of Durham. Comine's men have distributed themselves throughout the streets of the city and many Durham folk have been brutally murdered trying to resist the Norman take over. Comines is confident he can take control of Durham despite strong warnings from Aegelwine, the Bishop of Durham who has predicted his defeat.*

## January 31st 1069

### NORMANS MASSACRED IN DURHAM'S NARROW STREETS
*Early this morning the seven hundred strong army of Norman soldiers who seized the city of Durham yesterday were set upon by the Durham people aided by a large Northern army who broke open all the gates of Durham and stormed through the narrow streets of the city. Bodies of Norman soldiers were left strewn throughout the city streets while some Normans, including the leader Robert Comine fled for safety in the bishop's palace which was promptly set alight by the angry mob. For a time the severe blaze posed a great threat to the western tower of Durham's stone minster church but local people fell to their knees in prayer and miraculously the wind changed direction and diverted the flames away from the minster's tower.*

# BLOODBATH IN THE CITY

King William had good reason to fear Durham as the people of the city had little love for the Norman invaders. This was proved when a Norman army of seven-hundred men stormed into the City on January 30th 1069 under the command of an aggressive Norman earl by the name of Robert Comine.

Robert's men distributed themselves throughout the narrow streets of the city and were confident they could take control of the place despite strong warnings from the Bishop of Durham called Aegelwine who predicted their defeat.

The following morning the Bishop's prediction proved true as the Norman occupants of the city were set upon by the Durham people aided by a large Northumbrian army from the north who broke open all the gates of Durham and stormed through the narrow streets of the city, slaughtering the Normans as they went.

Some of the Normans, including Comine fled for safety to the bishop's palace but this was set alight causing a fierce blaze which posed a threat to the western tower of Durham's early stone minster. This caused great concern among the local people who in desperation fell to their knees;

> ......*with eyes filled with tears and elevated hands, petitioning heaven, that by some assistance of the holy saint the structure might be saved from damage.*

Miraculously the wind changed direction and diverted the flames away from the minster's tower. Comine and the occupants of the bishop's palace were burnt to death and the snow covered streets of the city, filled with the carcasses of dead soldiers are said to have ran with Norman blood. All but two of the Norman occupants lost their lives in the massacre.

King William was angered by the event and in the later part of 1069 sent north a second, even greater army to burn and plunder the land between York and Durham. This was known as the Harrying of the North. It demonstrated the might of the Norman army to the people of northern England and forced them to recognise Norman control. A chronicler recorded;

> *'Between York and Durham he did not leave a house standing. reducing the whole area by fire and sword, to a horrible desert smoking with blood and ashes.'*

# Cathedral

## CARILEPH'S CATHEDRAL

When William the Conqueror finally took control of Durham he appointed a Norman called William Walcher as Durham's first Prince Bishop by combining the powers of the Bishop with those of the Earl of Northumbria. The term 'Prince Bishop' did not actually come into use until many centuries later but it is a good description of the political and ecclesiastical powers of Walcher and succeeding Bishops of Durham.

Walcher's time as a Prince Bishop was characterised by weak leadership which ultimately resulted in him being murdered at Gateshead in 1081. He was replaced by a new bishop called William St Carileph who was the man responsible for building the present cathedral.

Carileph designed the greater part of the Cathedral of Durham as it stands today and began its construction in the year 1093. Occupying the site of the old stone minster built by Uchted, the new building was completed to the bishop's designs in more or less forty years. Unfortunately Carileph did not live to see the completion of his cathedral in 1135.

*The Nave*

## RIBBED VAULTING AND FLYING BUTTRESSES

The buildings of the Nave, the Choir and their accompanying aisles form the central body of the cathedral and it is these which were largely built to Carileph's designs in the period 1093 to 1135.

Inside the cathedral, the nave is particularly striking for its massive spiral and zig-zag decorated Cylindrical Piers (or columns) and the larger multiple columned Compound Piers which support the impressive diamond Ribbed Vaulting of the ceiling high above.

---

### January 31st 1069
**EARL DIES IN PALACE BLAZE**

*Robert Comine, the Earl of Northumbria and other Norman soldiers who took refuge in the bishop's palace during today's siege at Durham were burnt to death this morning as an angry mob of North Easterners set the building alight as protest against the Norman occupation of their sacred city. As the siege drew to a close the snow covered streets of the city were filled with the carcasses of dead soldiers. All but two of the Norman occupants lost their lives. These two lucky Norman soldiers escaped and will no doubt spend many years recalling the horrific events .*

### February 1st 1069
**EDGAR HEARS OF MASSACRE**
**Scotland**

*Edgar the Aethling of Wessex, the only remaining Anglo-Saxon claimant to the English throne has received news of the massacre of the Normans at Durham during his exile in Scotland. Edgar will be encouraged to challenge the Norman invaders.*

### September 1069
**MIRACLE FORCES RETREAT**
**Northallerton North Yorkshire**

*Norman soldiers from York have retreated at Northallerton during their march toward Durham which they intended to attack following the recent massacre of Norman soldiers in the city. The Durham folk claim that the Normans have been struck with fear by a sudden fog caused by the intervention of St Cuthbert who is said to have miraculous powers in the land north of Northallerton and the River Tees. The true reason for the retreat is more likely to be an invasion by a huge army of Danes who are sailing into Yorkshire by the Humber estuary. The Normans will have to deal with the invasion as priority.*

### December 1069
**MONKS TAKE REFUGE**
**Lindisfarne**

*The monkish Community of St Cuthbert have fled from Durham to escape the ravages of the Norman army. They have taken with them the body of their saint Cuthbert and will take temporary refuge on the Holy Island of Lindisfarne. The Durham monks were surprised by the receding tide which allowed them landward access to the island and proclaimed it a miracle of St Cuthbert. They were unaware that this is a regular natural occurrence.*

## December 1069

### BISHOP PLUNDERS DURHAM MINSTER

*The Community of St Cuthbert have returned to Durham from Lindisfarne with their saint's body after the recent attack by the Normans on the city. The environs of Durham have been severely destroyed by the Normans but perhaps the worst shock was to find that Aegelwine the Bishop of Durham had fled south and robbed the Durham minster of some of its richest treasures.*

## August 1072

### CASTLE BUILT

*William the Conqueror has ordered Earl Waltheof of Northumbria to build a castle at Durham City as an important defensive stronghold against the Scots. The king has appointed one of his own men William Walcher of Lorraine as the first non-Saxon Bishop of Durham.*

## 1075

### WALCHER BECOMES EARL-BISHOP

*Following the execution of Waltheof, the Earl of Northumbria who had plotted against the king, William Walcher the Norman Bishop of Durham has been given the extensive political powers formerly held by the Earl and has become a kind of `Earl-Bishop' or Prince Bishop of Durham with both political and ecclesisatical powers.*

## 1080

### MURDER BY BISHOP'S MEN
#### County Durham

*Liulf of Lumley an important Northumbrian nobleman and the first member of the Lumley family has been murdered by two of the Prince Bishop of Durham's men called Leobwin and Gilbert. Liulf has been a close confident of the Bishop and this has aroused much jealously among the bishop's men. The two retainers murdered Liulf and most of his family as they slept in their homes. Walcher the Bishop of Durham who had not consented to the murder has agreed to meet with remaining members of Liulf's family in an attempt to make peace.*

The Ribbed vaulting at Durham was in its time technically far more advanced than any vaulting to be found anywhere else in Britain or on the continent. In fact it is quite possible that Durham Cathedral was the first building in Europe to receive ribbed vaulting. The Cathedral at Durham is also important for the Flying Buttresses, a feature of pioneering development undertaken by the Norman masons at Durham. Situated in the Triforium or upper storey of the cathedral they can not be seen by visitors.

## PUDSEY'S CHAPEL AND ST BEDE'S TOMB

In later years two major additions were made to the cathedral of William St Carileph one of which was the Galilee Chapel built by Bishop Hugh Du Puiset, who was known more affectionately as Bishop Pudsey (1153-1195).

*The Galilee Chapel*

Pudsey's Galilee Chapel is at the western end of the cathedral and is situated right at the top of the gorge formed by the River Wear where it is overshadowed by the cathedral's twin towers. The Galilee Chapel is famous as the home of the black marble-topped tomb of The Venerable Bede (673-735 A.D), who was the first historian of England. Bede lived most of his life at Jarrow near the River Tyne. His bones were brought to Durham from the ruins of Jarrow monastery in the early eleventh century, when they were acquired by a relic collector. Bede's tomb is inscribed with the following Latin words

*Hac sunt in fossa Baedae Venerabilis Ossa*

Translated, this means ' in this tomb are of Bede the Bones'. Legend says that the use of the word Venerable is said to have been inspired into the mind of the writer of this poetic epitaph by an angel who told him how to complete the rhyme. The inscription dates from 1830.

The Galilee Chapel is also known as the Lady Chapel as it was once the only part of the cathedral that could be entered by women according to the rules of the Benedictine order of monks. A little way inside the main cathedral building we can see a line of black Frosterley Marble in the cathedral floor which marked the point beyond which women were not allowed to pass. So strict was the rule against women entering the cathedral that in 1333 when Queen Philippa, wife of Edward III crossed the line to find sleeping quarters in the cathedral, she was forced to sleep elsewhere. The Durham monks petitioned the king and insisted that she find sleeping accomodation in the castle to avoid upsetting St Cuthbert

Lady Chapels are normally constructed at the eastern end of cathedrals and not at the west so Durham is quite unusual in this respect. Initially there had been an attempt to build the Lady Chapel at the eastern end but problems with crumbling masonry forced Bishop Hugh Pudsey to transfer the building work to the west end.

The building problems are something of a mystery, but legend attributes the damage to St Cuthbert who is said to have disliked the idea of a Lady Chapel so close to the site of his tomb. At a later stage another chapel called the Chapel of the Nine Altars was built at the cathedral's east end - strangely this seems to have had no major structural problems.

# ROSE WINDOW CHAPEL

The huge Chapel of the Nine Altars at the eastern end of the cathedral was begun during the episcopacy of Bishop Richard le Poore (1228-1237) who was also associated with the building of Salisbury Cathedral. This new chapel provided more space for the increasing number of visiting pilgrims who packed the aisles and choir of the cathedral to view the shrine of St Cuthbert.

A number of interesting features can be seen in this chapel including some elegant piers of Frosterley Marble, a decorative black substance originating from the Durham valley of Weardale. It is embedded with the white shells of ancient sea creatures. Another prominent feature in the chapel is a large white statue of Bishop William Van Mildert who died in 1836.

Van Mildert, the last Prince Bishop of Durham was the man responsible for the foundation of Durham University in 1832. The University is of course the third oldest in England after Oxford and Cambridge.

Without doubt the most beautiful feature of the Chapel of the Nine Altars is the huge Rose Window which was originally made in the fifteenth century by Richard Pickering of Hemingbrough and reconstructed in the eighteenth century by James Wyatt. The Rose is ninety feet in circumference with a central core depicting Christ surrounded by the twelve apostles.

Inside the cathedral the Chapel of the Nine Altars lies just to the east of an elevated Feretory, (a chapel for saint's relics) in which we find the Tomb of St Cuthbert.

*May 15th 1080*
**BISHOP MURDERED AT GATESHEAD**
**Gateshead**

*William Walcher the Bishop of Durham was murdered at Gateshead yesterday by an angry mob of northerners protesting against the murder of Liulf of Lumley by the bishop's men. The Bishop had called for a meeting at Gateshead church but the angry mob led by one Eadulf Rus, drowned out the bishop's pleas for peace by chanting `Stout rede, good rede slay ye the bishop'. The bishop supported by around one hundred men took refuge in the church but the anger of the mob forced them to surrender the murderer Gilbert who was instructed to make peace. Gilbert was immediately killed before the mob set alight to the church. As the bishop tried to escape he was butchered to death. His body was found this morning in a terrible mutilated state by some monks from Jarrow, it will later be buried at Durham.*

*Late May 1080*
**MOB ATTACKS DURHAM**
*Following the recent murder of Bishop Walcher, an angry mob of northerners have been attacking the castle at Durham City which is a stronghold of the Normans in the north. The siege has been abandoned after four days of constant onslaught.*

*Summer 1080*
**FRENCH BISHOP ATTACKS NORTH**
*William the Conqueror has responded to the recent murder of Walcher the Bishop of Durham by sending north an army under the leadership of his brother Odo the Bishop of Bayeux. The Bishop's army has destroyed much of the land north of the Tees and the bishop himself stolen some valuable items from the monastery at Durham. Several of the Gateshead murderers who killed William Walcher and other Norman soldiers have fled to Scotland where they have been warmly welcomed by King Malcolm.*

## January 1081
### NEW BISHOP
*William of St Calais also known as William of St Carileph has been appointed as Bishop of Durham. The new bishop was consecrated at Gloucester in the presence of William the Conqueror. Bishop William was previously abbot of the monastery of St Vincent in Normandy. Carileph has not inherited the political powers held by his predecessor William Walcher who was an Earl-Bishop of Durham. A Norman called Aubrey de Coucy has inherited some political powers in the north as the new Earl of Northumbria.*

*Bishop Carileph's seal*

## 1083
### BISHOP REMOVES MONKS
*Bishop William St Carileph has removed the non celibate secular monks from the monastery of Durham minster and replaced them with a celibate order of monks under the leadership of the new prior called Aldwin. The non celibate monks have been removed to new monastic sites at Darlington,*

# THE SHRINE AND TOMB OF ST CUTHBERT

In medieval times Durham Cathedral was one of the greatest centres of pilgrimage in England and the chief reason for pilgrimage was the rich and glorious Shrine of St Cuthbert. Today the simple grey stone tomb inscribed 'Cuthbertus' is all that remains of the shrine but prior to the Dissolution of the Monasteries in the sixteenth century, the whole area around the tomb was an elaborately decorated shrine described as one of the richest monuments in England. Once decorated with an 'ingeniously made structure of costly green marble and gilded with gold' the shrine was bestowed with an incredible number of gifts and jewels including contributions from kings, queens, churchmen and wealthy nobles. These gifts were stored in beautifully decorated wainscot lockers which were situated on the north and south sides of the feretory. The lockers which also contained relics associated with St Cuthbert and other saints were opened for viewing on special occasions such as the feast day of St Cuthbert.

The magnificent shrine of St Cuthbert was destroyed in the sixteenth century along with many others throughout the land by the order of King Henry VIII. The men who opened St Cuthbert's tomb found a number of precious jewels and a wand of gold which were all confiscated by the crown.

# A SCREEN, A THRONE, A CLOCK AND THE TOWER

St Cuthbert's tomb and feretory are hidden from the Choir and the Nave to the west, by the magnificent fourteenth century Neville Screen which was at one time decorated with 107 alabaster figures. The screen was donated to the cathedral by John, the 5th Lord Neville (died 1388) and is constructed from Caen limestone originating from a French quarry many hundred miles away.

The massive screen was constructed in London and shipped north to Newcastle from where it was carried across land by cart to Durham. John Neville's tomb lies in the south aisle of the Nave where he is accompanied by his wife Matilda. The tomb of John's father Ralph Neville is also in the cathedral. It was Ralph who successfully led the English into victory over the Scots at the Battle of Nevilles Cross just outside Durham in 1346. As an honour for the victory he became the first layman to be allowed burial in the cathedral.

The south aisle of the cathedral choir contains the Tomb of Bishop Thomas Hatfield (1345-1381) who was bishop at the time of the Battle of Nevilles Cross. His tomb is covered by his alabaster effigy which lies snugly tucked under a decorated arch formed by a short stairway leading to the Bishops' Throne or 'Cathedra' directly above. The Bishop's throne at Durham is the highest in Christendom.

To the west of the choir we stand directly beneath the Central Tower which was built in the fifteenth century. An earlier tower had been destroyed by lightning in 1429. The entrance to the cathedral tower is in the South Transept where we find the sixteenth century decorated Cathedral Clock

During the Civil War when 4000 Scottish prisoners were held in the cathedral following the Battle of Dunbar (1650) nearly all the woodwork in the great church was destroyed by the

Scottish prisoners for firewood. The clock was spared, seemingly because it has a carving of the sacred Scottish thistle upon it.

# THE CLOISTERS, PLACE OF THE MONKS

To the south of, but adjoining the cathedral are the buildings of the Cloisters which are clustered around a small square green called the Cloister Garth. The buildings surrounding the garth were the monastic priory buildings of the cathedral and include the Chapter House, the Monk's Dormitory, the Refectory and the Great Kitchen.

Around the square green are four covered Cloister walkways where the monks spent considerable periods of time during the heyday of the Durham priory. One of the walkways on the northern side of the cloisters, by the main cathedral wall was formerly the monk's Scriptorium. This contained a number of reading chambers in which the monks could study.

At the western end of this walkway a plaque can be seen informing American tourists that a distant relation of George Washington was a prior at Durham Cathedral. The Washingtons were an old County Durham family originating from Washington near Sunderland.

Above the western walkway of the Cloister is the Monks' dormitory, the site of the monkish sleeping quarters. It dates from the fourteenth century and has an extremely impressive roof of wooden oak beams. It now houses a library belonging to the Dean and Chapter and has a collection of Anglo-Saxon and Viking crosses from throughout the ancient kingdom of Northumbria.

On the opposite side of the cloisters we find the Chapter House where meetings are held to discuss the day to day running of the cathedral. The building contains the tombs of three very important Bishops of Durham - William St Carileph, Ranulf Flambard and Hugh Du Puiset. Above the southern walkway of the cloisters was situated the Refectory or eating area. This is now a private library belonging to the Dean and Chapter. Behind the refectory is the peculiar octagonal shaped building of the Kitchen.

# BOOKS AND RELICS

Today most visitors to the cloisters are drawn to the cathedral's restaurant, the bookshop and the Treasury Museum which all lie in the south western corner of the cloisters. The Treasury Museum is one of the most important museums in the north of England and contains many relics of the 'Golden Age of Northumbria'.

The museum's ancient exhibits include the 7th century wooden Coffin of St Cuthbert which has been carefully pieced together and the Pectoral Cross of St Cuthbert. Some very impressive silver plate may also be seen in the museum which belonged to the Prince Bishops of Durham. Other interesting items include some ancient books and the sword called the Conyer's Falchion which is said to have been used by Sir John Conyers in the killing of the legendary 'Sockburn Worm' close to the village of Croft on Tees near Darlington.

The sword is presented to each new Bishop of Durham on entering the diocese of Durham for the first time at Croft Bridge. It is a great ceremonial tradition in which a local dignitary declares; 'My lord bishop I hereby present you with the falchion wherewith the champion

Norton near Stockton and St Helens Auckland. The new monks at Durham have been brought in from Monkwearmouth and Jarrow.

*November 14th 1088*
**BISHOP FLEES TO FRANCE**
*William of St Carileph the Bishop of Durham and Robert de Mowbray the new Earl of Northumberland have supported the claims of Robert Curthose, the eldest son of William the Conqueror to the English throne. These two important northern figures join Odo the Bishop of Bayeux and many others on a long list accused of favouring Curthose as king. Bishop William has fled to Normandy after his castle at Durham was besieged by Ivo Tallebois and Erneis de Buron who are Norman supporters of King William. The bishopric of Durham has been left vacant.*

*1088*
**PRIOR HAS SCOTTISH CONNECTIONS**
*The new prior of Durham is Turgot a monk from Dunfermeline abbey. He has taken over the administration of the bihsopric of Durham following the recent departure of Bishop William of St Carileph who has fled to Normandy after his alleged involvement in a plot to remove King William Rufus. Turgot could be a very dangerous or a very useful appointment for King William as he has connections with the court of King Malcolm of Scotland. Turgot is also the confessor to Queen Margaret the Scottish queen.*

*September 14th 1091*
**BISHOP BUYS POLITICAL RIGHTS**
*William of St Carileph has been restored to the bishopric of Durham at the end of his three year exile. The king has given the bishop similar political powers in the north to those bestowed on his predecessor Walcher although he is likely to be a shrewder politician than the murdered bishop. Many of the powers bestowed to Bishop Carileph of Durham by King William Rufus have been bought by the Bishop from Robert De Mowbray, the Earl of Northumberland. The Earl of Northumberland has held certain political rights in the land between the Tyne and Tees which form part of the Earldom of Northumbria. These rights have been bought by Bishop Carileph with the encouragement of King William Rufus. Only the very southern portion of County Durham called Sadberge remains the territory of the Earl.*

## 1091
### PRINCE BISHOP'S POWERS
*The politcial powers of the Bishop of Durham are confined mainly to land between the Tyne and Tees with pockets of teritory further north in Northumberland. Bishop Carileph's politcial territory is called a Palatine and in his capacity as a virtual ruler over this land he can be described as a 'Prince Bishop'. As 'Prince Bishop' Carileph and his successors will have powers enabling them to hold their own parliament, raise their own armies, appoint their own sherriffs and justices, administer their own laws, levy taxes and customs duties, create fairs and markets, issue charters, salvage shipwrecks, collect revenue from mines, administer forests and mint their own coins.*

## August 11th 1093
### NEW CATHEDRAL FOR DURHAM
*The construction of a Norman cathedral at Durham has been commenced by Bishop William of St Carileph who has demolished the older Saxon minster to make way for a magnificent new building. Bishop William is inspired by the new churches he has seen during his exile in Normandy and is aiming to build something of great magnificence. The first three stones of the building were laid by Bishop William St Carileph, King Malcolm of Scotland and Prior Tugot of Durham.*

## January 6th 1096
### ACCUSED BISHOP DIES
**Windsor**

*William of St Carileph, the Bishop of Durham who instigated the building of a new cathedral at Durham has died at Windsor where he has been summoned to meet the king on suspicion of involvement in an attempt to overthrow the monarch. He has not lived to see the completion of his cathedral at Durham which is still under construction.*

## 1099
### CUNNING FLAMBARD IS NEW BISHOP
*Ranulf Flambard has become the new Bishop of Durham. He is a minister to King William Rufus and has greatly pleased the king as his chief adviser. Flambard had postponed appointments to*

Conyers slew the worm, dragon or fiery flying serpent which destroyed man, woman and child in memory of which the king then reigning gave him the manor of Sockburn to hold by this tenure that upon the entrance of every bishop into the county the falchion sould be presented'.

The rectory at Croft where Lewis Caroll lived as a boy overlooks the bridge where the sword is presented. The dragon legend may have inspired him to write the Jabberwocky, a famous dragon slaying rhyme he wrote at Croft on Tees and Whitburn near Sunderland.

> *'And, as in uffish thought he stood, The Jabberwock with eyes of flame came whiffling through the tulgey wood and burbled as it came!. One, two! One, two! and through and through, the vorpal blade went snicker-snack!, he left it dead and with its head, he went galumphing back.'.*
>
> Lewis Carroll

# SANCTUARY

Most visitors to the Cathedral will have entered the building from Palace Green by the North Door on which we find the imposing bronze Sanctuary Knocker. This is a near perfect replica of the twelfth century original which can be seen in the Treasury Museum. It features the face of a hideous lion-like beast and represents the ancient privelege of sanctuary once granted to criminal offenders at Durham cathedral.

Criminals could seek refuge at Durham by loudly banging the knocker to alert the attentions of the watchers who resided in two small chambers overlooking the door. A watcher would then invite the criminal inside the cathedral.

Upon entering the cathedral the criminal had to exchange his clothes for a black robe with a yellow cross of St Cuthbert imprinted on the left shoulder. He would then confess the details of his crime before a coroner and was allowed to remain inside the cathedral for a period of thirty seven days. Here he was provided with food and water paid for by the church. Before or on the thirty seventh day the criminal was expected to leave the country by an assigned port or else face execution. In the case of Durham the assigned port was usually Hartlepool

The criminals were escorted to the sea port by the constables of each parish they passed through. On no account was the criminal allowed to stray from the King's highway during the journey as this was punishable by death. Offenders seeking sanctuary at Durham came from every part of the country and included burglars, cattle stealers and horse thieves. More usually the offence was murder.

bishoprics including Durham and enforced heavy feudal payments from barons. This earned much extra revenue for the king who has awarded Flambard with the bishopric of Durham, although there is some suggestion that Flambard may have paid a small fee for the purchase of the bishopric.

## 1100
### BISHOP IMPRISONED
**London**

*Ranulf Flambard the Bishop of Durham, a chief adviser to the late King William Rufus has been imprisoned in the Tower of London by Henry I following advice from council. Flambard has many enemies in the country who will be pleased to see him locked up.*

## February 1101
### BISHOP ESCAPES
**London**

*Ranulf Flambard the Bishop of Durham has escaped from the Tower of London by means of a rope smuggled in to him by some unknown person. Flambard has fled to France to seek refuge with his friend Robert Curthose, the Duke of Normandy.*

## July 1101
### BISHOP SUPPORTS INVASION OF ENGLAND

*Ranulf Flambard the Bishop of Durham has persuaded the king's brother, Robert Curthose, Duke of Normandy to invade England. King Henry has backed down from confrontation with Robert in Hampshire and has agreed to pay for the Duke's expedition and grant pardons to all the duke's allies. Ranulf Flambard has been restored to the Bishopric of Durham.*

## September 1104
### SAINT BURRIED IN CATHE-DRAL

*St Cuthbert's body was finally laid to rest in Durham Cathedral this month. The body had been temporarily laid in a nearby chapel while the construction work on the great cathedral was undertaken. During the movement of the corpse, the body was inspected by ten monks who found the body to be whole and incorrupt with a fragrant smell. It is thought that the body was embalmed.*

## June 1107
### PRIOR BECOMES A SCOTTISH BISHOP
**Fife Scotland**

*Turgot, the prior at Durham Cathedral monastery has become the new Bishop of St Andrews in Fife. Turgot was one of the men present at the laying of Durham Cathedral's first stones in 1093.*

## 1112
### FLAMBARD BUILDS HOSPITAL
*St Giles Church and the hospital of Kepier have been founded in Durham City by Bishop Ranulf Flambard.*

## 1115
### BISHOP GIVES FINCHALE TO SAINT
*St Godric has been granted land at Finchale near Durham City by Bishop Ranulf Flambard. Godric intends to establish a hermitage at this beautiful spot by the River Wear.*

## 1121
### PRINCE BISHOP RAIDS SCOT-LAND
**Scotland**

*Flambard the Prince Bishop of Durham has attacked Scotland with an army of his men using his newly fortified site of Norham on Tweed as a base.*

## 1128
### CITY BRIDGE BUILT
*Framwellgate Bridge has been constructed linking the city by road with the north. The bridge built by the Prince Bishop Ranulf Flambard has excellent views of Durham Castle and the cathedral which is nearing completion.*

### 1128
**FLAMBARD DIES**

Ranulf Flambard the Bishop of Durham has died after twenty nine years as bishop. The bishop who had made many enemies during his life had tried in vain to make up for the wrongs of his earlier life by restoring priveleges taken from the Durham monks.

### 1132
**CATHEDRAL COMPLETE**

Durham Cathedral has been completed. The cathedral has been built largely to the designs of Bishop William of St Carileph who died in 1096.

### 1133
**RUFUS IS NEW BISHOP**

The new Bishop of Durham is Geoffrey Rufus the king's chancellor who was consecrated as the new Bishop of Durham in York today by Thurstan, Archbishop of York. Bishop Rufus is the successor to Ranulf Flambard who died in 1128.

### 1135
**MINT ESTABLISHED**

The Bishop's mint has been establihed near to Durham Castle. Unique Durham coins will be produced here.

### February 5th 1136
**PEACE TREATY SIGNED IN DURHAM**

King Stephen of England and David King of Scotland have signed a treaty at Durham in an attempt to settle land disputes. David's son Henry has been granted the Earldom of Huntingdon but King Stephen will keep Northumberland which has been claimed by the Scots for many years.

### 1141
**USURPER SEIZES BISHOP'S CASTLE**

A usurper is claiming to be the Prince Bishop of Durham following the death of Bishop Geoffrey. William Cumin who has been a loyal if somewhat devious chaplain to the bishop has seized the bishop's castle with the support of several of the bishop's servants. Cumin is a usurper with no right to the bishop's throne, the only royal support he has for his claim is from King David of Scotland. Cumin has forged papal documents claiming that he is the new Bishop of Durham but the monks of

Durham cathedral monastery have refused to accept him.

## 1143
### MONKS ELECT BISHOP
**York City**

William St Barbara has become the official Bishop of Durham despite the claims of the usurper William Cumin. Some monks escaped to Rome to clarify whether or not Cumin had any right to the bishopric. The pope has instructed them that Cumin is not a bishop and ordered that the monks elect a new bishop within forty days. William of St Barbara, the Dean of York has been elected to the Prince Bishop's post. The new bishop has been consecrated at Winchester.

## 1144
### USURPER CAPTURED
**Kirk Merrington**

William Cumin the usurper bishop of Durham has been captured by Durham barons with the assistance of the Earl of Northumberland at Kirk Merrington.

## May 1154
### PUDSEY IS BISHOP

Hugh du Puiset also known as Hugh de Puteaco (known as Bishop Pudsey) has been elected the new Bishop of Durham by the Durham monks following the death of William of St Barbara last year. Pudsey who is only twenty five is a nephew of King Stephen and reputedly a great grandson of William the Conqueror. Pudsey, who has been treasurer of York and Archdeacon of Winchester will be thought by many to be too young for the job but the new bishop has visited the Pope in Rome to be consecrated before returning to Durham for his enthronement this month.

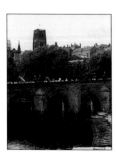

## 1160
### ELVET BRIDGE BUILT
Bishop Hugh Pudsey has built a stone bridge across the River Wear in Durham.

*Finchale Priory*

## 1170
### SAINT DIES AGED 105
**Finchale**

*St Godric of Finchale has died at the age of 105. Godric who was born somewhere in Norfolk in 1065 spent the early part of his life as a pedlar and sea pirate on the open seas until a pilgrimage to Compostella in Spain made him decide to become a hermit. For a time he settled at Carlisle where he established a hermitage before moving to Wolsingham in Weardale where he lived in a cave before finally settling at Finchale, persuading the Bishop of Durham Ranulf Flambard to allow him to build a hermitage.*

## 1171
### BISHOP'S NEPHEW LANDS AT HARTLEPOOL
**Hartlepool**

*Count Hugh de Barr, the nephew of Hugh Pudsey, the Bishop of Durham has brought a fleet of ships into the natural harbour of Hartlepool to assist William King of Scotland in his invasion of England. It is highly likely that Bishop Pudsey has encouraged his nephew to assist in this way*

## July 1174
### REBEL FLEET RETURNS HOME
**Hartlepool**

*The fleet of Count Hugh de Barr, the nephew of Pudsey the Bishop of Durham has returned to Flanders after hearing of the capture of William the King of Scotland at Alnwick.*

## 1174
### LADY CHAPEL BUILT
*The Galilee Chapel has been built at Durham Cathedral by Bishop Hugh Pudsey for the use of*

ladies, who are not presently allowed to enter the building. As a lady chapel the Galilee is unusual in its situation at the western end of the cathedral, as Lady chapels are normally constructed at the eastern end of cathedral buildings. Strangely, attempts have been made at Durham to build a lady chapel at the eastern end of the Cathedral but the foundations collapsed. Some believe the miracle working St Cuthbert is raising an objection to the presence of women near his tomb at the eastern end of the building.

## 1179

### CITY CHARTER
The Bishop of Durham, Hugh Pudsey has granted Durham a charter for a market. The charter is 'retrospective' and allows markets, fairs and other freedoms in the city of Durham. A market is thought to have existed in Durham since 1040.

## 1179

### POPE CONFIRMS CHARTER
Durham's Charter has been confirmed by the Pope in a Papal Bull. (Beverley is the only other borough in England known to have received a papal bull confirming its charter).

## 1180

### HOUSES IN OLD ELVET
A new borough called Elvet Haugh (Old Elvet) has been established by the Bishop of Durham on land belonging to the Durham Priory. The new borough consists of forty merchants' houses and is linked to the city by Elvet Bridge.

## 1181

### PUDSEY BUILDS HOSPITAL
Sherburn Hospital has been constructed by Bishop Pudsey near Durham City

*Sherburn Hospital*

**WELCOME TO THE WORLD**

The City of Durham offers investors and visitors a rich combination of the old and the new.

The historic City with a World Heritage Site at its centre, an internationally acclaimed University, modern industrial estates and a new Science Park uniquely combines tradition, culture and technology.

The result is a first class business culture, a renowned tourist destination and an unrivalled quality of life.

To find out more about the benefits of the City of Durham why not contact the Economic Development Unit on Tel: (0191) 386 6111, Fax: (0191) 386 0625.

CITY of DURHAM
ECONOMIC • DEVELOPMENT • UNIT

### 1183
**DURHAM DOMESDAY**

*Hugh Pudsey, the Bishop of Durham has carried out a survey of all his territory in Durham and in parts of Northumberland. The survey known as the Boldon Buke is Durham's equivalent of the Domesday Book which was instigated by King William the Conqueror in 1086. Durham, Northumberland, Cumberland and Westmorland were not included in King William the Conqueror's famous survey.*

### 1228
**DURHAM GETS POORE**

*Richard le Poore has been appointed as the new Bishop of Durham*

### 1233
**TOWER BUILT**

*The Central Tower has been built at Durham Cathedral. The tower is one of the last major additions to the Cathderal building along with the Chapel of the Nine altars which is now under construction.*

### 1237
**TIGHTROPE TRAGEDY**

*A man employed by the Prior of Durham to entertain the monks fell to his death while walking on a tightrope stretched between the central tower and a western tower of Durham Cathedral. King Henry III hearing of this prank, has informed the prior that he has now destroyed all his chances of becoming the next Bishop of Durham.*

### 1242
**CHAPEL COMPLETE**

*The Chapel of the Nine Altars has been completed at Durham Cathedral.*

### 1283
**ARCHBISHOP KICKED OUT**

*The Archbishop of York has been kicked out of Durham by Durham monks angry at his attempts to inspect their wealthy monastery. The Archbishop was visting Durham before the appointment of the new Bishop in the city. The monks indignantly clipped the tail of the Archbishop's horse and chased him out of the city's market place by a narrow alley near St Nicholas Church.*

## 1284
### BISHOP ORDERED TO EXCOMMUNICATE MONKS
*The Archbishop of York has ordered the newly appointed Bishop of Durham, Anthony Bek to excommunicate the Durham monks who humiliated the archbishop on his recent visit to Durham. Bek has refused the Archbishop's orders.*

## 1284
### EXCOMMUNICATION OVERTHROWN BY KING
*The Archbishop of York has failed in an attempt to excommunicate Anthony Bek, the Bishop of Durham who has refused to take orders from the senior churchman. Bek claimed that as Prince Bishop he could only take orders from the king. The king naturally agreed and the excommuncation has been ovethrown.*

## 1284
### CROOK HALL BUILT
*Peter Del Croke has built a manor house close to the banks of the River Wear at Durham*

## 1298
### BISHOP JOINS BATTLE AGAINST SCOTS
**Falkirk**

*An English army have attacked Scotland and were victorious at the Battle of Falkirk. The English army has included the services of Anthony Bek, the Bishop of Durham*

## 1298
### KING ENTERTAINED
**Kepier near Durham**

*King Edward I was entertained at Kepier Hospital near the banks of the River Wear in Durham.*

## May 1300
### BISHOP DEMANDS ACCESS TO PRIORY
*Anthony Bek, the Bishop of Durham has demanded an official visitation to the priory of Durham which lies adjacent to the cathedral. The prior Richard de Hoton has refused, so Bek has imprisoned the Durham monks in the priory.*

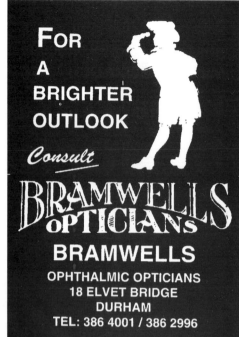

*Shincliffe*

### June 18th 1300
**BISHOP'S MEN ATTACK PRIOR**
*King Edward has met with the monks of Durham and promised to settle their dispute with the Bishop of Durham. The prior of Durham was recently attacked at Shincliffe by retainers of the Bishop.*

### 1311
**KELLAW BECOMES BISHOP**
*Richard Kellaw of Kelloe near Durham has been appointed the new Bishop of Durham*

### 1312
**ROBERT THE BRUCE ATTACKS DURHAM**
*The Scots under Robert the Bruce have severely burned and plundered the outskirts of Durham in a raid which has taken them as far south as Hartlepool, a place closely associated with Robert's ancestors.*

### 1318
**MURDER ON THE BRIDGE**
*The Bishop of Durham's steward Richard Fitzmarmaduke has been murdered by his cousin Robert Neville on Framwellgate Bridge.*

### 1323
**WALLS RESTORED**
*The historic city walls of Durham have undergone restoration this year. The walls have provided an invaluable defence against the raiding Scots.*

## 1333

### QUEEN ASKED TO LEAVE CATHEDRAL

*King Edward III has stayed at Durham Cathedral before his March into Northumberland to fight against the Scots. Queen Philippa was asked to leave the cathedral and sleep in the castle to avoid upsetting St Cuthbert who is thought to have disliked women.*

## 1342

### SCOTS RAID CITY

*Durham City has been severely raided by the Scots and many of the city's residents have been killed. The attack followed a failure by the Scots to penetrate the city walls of Newcastle which forced them to turn their attentions elsewhere.*

*Bishop Hatfield's Seal*

## 1345

### NEW BISHOP

*Thomas Hatfield has been appointed Bishop of Durham*

## October 17th 1346

### BATTLE AT NEVILLES CROSS

*The Scots under David II attacked the priories at Hexham and Blanchland before making their way south to attack the City of Durham today. At first the main Scottish army assembled at Beau repaire (Bearpark) while foraging parties plundered the western hills. Eventually the main Scottish and English forces engaged in battle on the Red Hills near Nevilles Cross on the western outskirts of the city. The Scots are said to have outnumbered the English but they were heavily defeated. After the battle, the Scottish King David was discovered hiding under the arch of Aldin Grange Bridge on the River Browney not far from Neville's Cross. The king is to be imprisoned and held for ransom.*

# astle & the Baileys

## THE BISHOP'S FORT

Durham Castle is the ancient palace of the Prince Bishops of Durham and lies at the northern end of Palace Green opposite the cathedral. It is situated on the site of a fortress built to the orders of William the Conqueror on his return from Scotland in 1072. Waltheof, the Saxon Earl of Northumberland undertook the work of building the castle for William but over the years a succession of Prince Bishops have added important sections to the great building.

*Durham Castle in the Eighteenth Century*

The present castle is dominated by the keep which although the most imposing part of the castle is in fact the least historic. In the tradition of the Norman Motte and Bailey castles the keep is situated on a mound and was first erected in the fourteenth century during the episcopacy of Bishop Thomas Hatfield. Over the centuries the keep fell into a ruinous state but was rebuilt in the 1840s as a sleeping quarters for students when the castle became Durham's University College.

---

### 1354
**THE MINER MONKS**
**Ferryhill and Rainton**

*The monks of Durham have leased a coal mine at Ferryhill . They already own a mine at Rainton, west of Durham.*

### 1371
**BISHOP'S THRONE BUILT**
*The Bishop of Durham's Throne or 'Cathedra' has been built at Durham Cathedral*

### 1375
**NEVILLE SCREEN BROUGHT TO CATHEDRAL**
*The beautiful Neville Screen has been erected in Durham Cathedral. Shipped from Caen in France the screen was brought to Durham in sections from Newcastle by cart.*

### 1414
**NEW SCHOOL**
*Durham School has been established in the city.*

### 1416
**PLAGUED BY THE PLAGUE**
*An outbreak of plague has hit the city of Durham. (It will continue in the city for five years.)*

### 1417
**GATE BUILT**
*Bishop Langley has built The Great North Gate, an important fortification situated between Saddler Street and the North Bailey.*

### March 28th 1424
**HOSTAGES EXCHANGED**
*James King of Scotland, a prisoner in England has been given freedom. King James was exchanged for English hostages in the City of Durham. A peace treaty called the Treaty of Durham lasting for seven years has been signed by the King and has been witnessed by Langley Bishop of Durham, the Bishop of London, Lord Dacre, Lord Greystock, Richard Neville, and Sir Robert Umfraville. King James, after spending a month under the hospitality of the Bishop of Durham was escorted to the abbey of Melrose in Scotland where the treaty was confirmed*

*1429*

**TOWER HIT BY LIGHTNING**

*After a dreadful storm, a bolt of lightning hit the belfry tower of Durham cathderal today, causing a fire which continued to burn for several hours before twenty feet of the upper part of the belfry fell down. The tower will be rebuilt.*

*1438*

**CLOISTERS BUILT**

*The monastic cloister buildings have been erected at Durham Cathedral. Meanwhile the new bishop Robert Neville has erected an exchequer building on Palace Green.*

*September 26th 1448*

**KING MAKES PILGRIMAGE TO DURHAM**

*King Henry IV has made a visit to the shrine of St Cuthbert in Durham Cathedral. He has stayed for three days before returning south.*

*1451*

**CHAPEL BUILT AT GILESGATE**

*The Chapel of St Mary Magdalene has been built near Gilesgate in Durham City.*

*1486*

**MONKS MINE BELOW DRAINAGE LEVEL**

**Moorhouse near Rainton**

*The first recorded coal mining beneath the level of free drainage in Durham is taking place at Moorhouse Close near the city. The monks of Finchale have had to provide a new pump in order to mine in the area.*

*July 23rd 1503*

**KING'S DAUGHTER STAYS AT DURHAM**

*Margaret Tudor, the eldest daughter of Henry VII who is due to marry the King of Scotland, has stayed at Durham where she was entertained by Bishop Fox in the Great Hall of the castle.*

The older and greater part of the castle is situated around a courtyard to the west of the keep. The courtyard is entered from the gatehouse near to the site of the castle moat. The moat, a dry moat, was crossed by means of a draw bridge just outside the Gatehouse. Primarily the work of Bishop Pudsey (1153-1195), the Gatehouse underwent some alterations during the episcopacies of Bishop Tunstal (1530-1559) and Bishop Shute Barrington (1791-1826).

## A HALL AND A KITCHEN

Passing through the castle gatehouse into the courtyard, the imposing Keep may be seen to the right while to the left is the thirteenth and fourteenth century Great Hall built by Bishop Anthony Bek (1284-1311) and Bishop Thomas Hatfield (1345-1381). The nearest part of this building includes a five hundred year old kicthen built by Bishop Fox around 1500. Fox's coat of arms can be seen in the Tudor style woodwork of the adjacent hatch in the Buttery and depicts a Pelican piercing its breast to feed its young. Coats of Arms associated with various other Prince Bishops of Durham can be seen throughout the castle.

Most of the Great Hall building is occupied by the impressive Dining Hall of Bishop Bek which is about 100 feet long and 45 feet high. It serves as the Dining Hall for University College Durham and compares very well with the great dining halls of Oxford and Cambridge.

Inside, the western and northern wings of the castle are adjoined by the Black Staircase of Bishop Cosin. Dating from 1662, it is one of the most impressive staircases of its time in England. The castle's North wing was the site of a hall built by Bishop Pudsey but a number of alterations were made by successive bishops and this part of the castle now includes the Bishop's suite, the Bishop's Dining Room, the Tunstal Gallery and the Senate Room.

## PALACE GREEN

Palace Green separates the castle from the cathedral which lies at the southern end of the green. Until the twelfth century during the time of Bishop Flambard this area was the centre of Durham and the site of the old market place. It contained a mass of wooden houses huddled together between the castle and the cathedral until Flambard cleared them all to remove the potential fire hazard which threatened the castle and cathedral. The area thus became an open green as it it is today.

Today the green is flanked on its east and west sides by a number of historic buildings dating mainly from the eighteenth century. Most of these now belong to Durham University and include part of the University Library. Other buildings include Bishop Cosin's Hall (formerly Archdeacon Inn) and Bishops Cosin's Almshouse of 1666. On the western side of the green, near the Cathedral's western towers is a former Grammar School, now the University Music School. The Grammar School was reputedly haunted by a young pupil who suffered a fatal punishment from one of his masters who apparently threw him from a balcony in a fit of anger.

# THE FULLING MILL AND PREBENDS BRIDGE

From the western side of Palace Green a narrow lane called Windy Gap leads to the wooded river bank and the famous Fulling Mill. Once the property of the Priors of Durham, the Fulling Mill was known historically as the Jesus Mill. Today it is the home of the University Museum of Archaeology which houses relics of the region's Anglo-Saxon and Roman past.

A little to the south of the Fulling Mill is the Prebends Bridge of 1777 from where the best known view of Durham Cathedral can be obtained with the Cathedral's Western Towers majestically overlooking the wooded river bank and Fulling Mill below. It was this view that prompted Sir Walter Scott to write the following famous lines

*'Grey towers of Durham- yet well I love thy mixed and massive piles- half church of God; half castle 'gainst the Scot; And long to roam these venerable aisles, with records stored of deeeds long since forgot'*

The name of Prebends Bridge derives from the office of a Prebendary which is an honourary canon but the name pre-bend could be applied to its situation at the point where the River Wear bends to form the tip of the Durham peninsula. This area is known as 'Counts Corner' and is so named from the proximity of a little Grecian style folly nearby called 'The Count's House' which is said to be the old home of a tiny Polish Count called Joseph Borruwlawski.

## THE BAILEYS

In days gone by the fifty-eight acre Durham river peninsula was surrounded by the defensive city walls linked to the castle. Throughout the Middle ages the whole peninsula was known as 'the castle' so that the cathedral arguably lay within the castle!.

Just enclosed within the castle walls on the eastern side was the castle bailey which took the form of a street. The street still exists - part is called the South Bailey the other part the North Bailey. The North and South Baileys are among the most historic and most attractive streets of Durham City and are described by the architectural historian Sir Nicholas Pevsner as the best streets in Durham. In Early times the houses in the North and South Bailey were of great importance as they were held by military tenants employed to defend the city of Durham from attack.

## 1540
### HENRY DISSOLVES THE MONASTERY
*Durham Cathedral Monastery has been dissolved along with many other northern monasteries by King Henry VIII.*

*Bishop James Pilkington*

## 1561
### FIRST PROTESTANT BISHOP AT DURHAM
*James Pilkington has become the first protestant Bishop of Durham. The new bishop has removed all superstitious books and statues of idolatry from the cathedral.*

## January 30th 1565
### BISHOP'S CHARTER
*Bishop Pilkington has issued a charter of incorporation for the citizens of Durham and Framwellgate.*

## 1569
### REBELS FAIL TO OVERTHROW QUEEN
**Brancepeth**

*The two most powerful families in northern England, the Nevilles of Durham and Percys of Northumberland, have plotted to overthrow Queen Elizabeth I and reinstate Roman Catholocism in what has become known as 'The Rising of the North'. The rising, which gained huge support, was plotted at Brancepeth and Raby Castles but has been a failure. Brancepeth and Raby have been confiscated from the Nevilles by the Crown. Sixty persons were executed at Durham for their part in the rising. There were many other executions throughout the north in nearly every town and village from Wetherby to Newcastle.*

## 1583

### APOSTLE KILLED BY OX

*Bernard Gilpin, known as the 'Apostle of the North' has been killed by an ox in Durham City. Gilpin, who was 66 and a 'tall and lean person with a hawk like nose', played a great part in spreading the word of God among the rough and troublesome border folk of Northumberland.*

## 1589

### PLAGUE HITS DURHAM

*Plague has ravaged the north and forced many of the poorer residents of Durham City to move out to Elvet Moor, where an arrangement of cells have been constructed for their occupation. In the previous year 1,726 had been killed by plague in Newcastle.*

## 1590

### PRIESTS EXECUTED

*Three Roman Catholic priests have been executed at Durham. They are among the first of many executed throughout the reign of Elizabeth I, who has forbid Roman Catholic Priests from practising in the country.*

## 1592

### GYPSIES HANGED

*Five men have been hanged at Dryburn, Durham City, on suspicion that they might be gypsies. The parish register of St Nicholas has recorded their names as Arrrington, Fetherstone, Fenwick, Lancaster and Simson.*

## 1594

### CATHOLICS EXECUTED

*John Speed, a layman has been executed at Durham for assisting Roman Catholic priests. John Bost a Roman Catholic priest has also been executed in the city. Similar executions have taken place at Gateshead and Darlington.*

## 1597

### PLAGUE KILLS EIGHT HUNDRED IN CITY

*The plague has once again ravaged the north Newcastle, Darlington, Aycliffe, and Chester-le-Street have all been badly hit. By October 17, 340 people had died of plague at Darlington. In Durham City the death toll reached 844 on October 27th. The figures for each Durham City parish were as*

# THE CHAMPION BOXER

Most of the present houses of the North and South Bailey are of Georgian origin and in the eighteenth century these two streets were very fashionable town houses for County Durham's wealthiest landowners. The residents included the Earls of Strathmore, (The Bowes Family) who were ancestors of the present Royal family and the Coal owning Liddell family whose relatives included Alice Liddell, the inspiration for Lewis Carroll's 'Alice in Wonderland'. Alice's great grandmother lived in the South Bailey.

Other former residents of the Bailey included a certain Captain Boulby who fought at Waterloo, Sir Robert Ker Porter, an artist to the Tsar of Russia who later married a Russian princess and the little Polish Count called Joseph Borruwlawski

One famous nineteenth century resident of the Bailey was John Gully, who settled at Durham in the later part of his life. A one time champion pugilist of all England, Gully learned to fight during a period of imprisonment for debt at Bristol. He had the good fortune to be bought out of prison by a group of wealthy sportsmen on condition that he agreed to box against a notorious undefeated champion fighter called Henry the 'Game Chicken' Pearce.

Gully was defeated in the match against Pearce but only after the fight had gone a staggering fifty-nine rounds on October 8th 1805. It was not long after that Pearce retired and Gully went on to become the champion of all England by defeating another great boxer called 'The Lancashire Giant'.

During his eventful life Gully not only established himself as a great boxer but was for a time a member of Parliament (for Pontefract) and also a very successful horse owner, winning the Derby on two occasions.

In County Durham he invested his wealth in collieries at Trimdon, Hetton and Thornley. It was in 1863 at his house at number 7 the North Bailey, that Gully finally died at the age of 80. He left behind him twenty-four children from two successive marriages.

# THE GREAT NORTH GATE

In times gone by the North Bailey was divided from the South Bailey by a defensive wall through which the road passed by means of a gateway called Bow Church Gate. This was situated close to the church of St Mary le Bow which takes its name from the archway of the old gate. The church is now the Durham Heritage Centre.

Bow Church Gate was one of a number of gates that pierced the old city walls of Durham but the most impressive of them all was The Great North Gate which stood at the top of the North Bailey where it joined Saddler Street.

First built around 1072 and adjoining the castle to the west, it played a very important part in controlling the movement of traffic into the peninsula area. In the early fifteenth century the building was largely rebuilt by Bishop Langley to accomodate the city jail. For the next four-hundred years it served a joint purpose of gateway and prison. In the later days of its life it was known as the 'Jail Gates'.

John Howard, a prison reformer visited this jail in 1774 and described its conditions;

*The North Gate*

*'The men are put at night into dungeons, one seven feet square for three prisoners another the 'Great Hole' has only a little window. In this I saw six prisoners most of them transports chained to the floor in that situation they had been for many weeks and were very sick'*

In 1819 prisoners were moved to the new prison at Elvet and the next year the Great North Gate was removed because of the difficulties it presented to coaches passing into the bailey.

follows; Elvet 400 dead, St Nicholas (Market Place) 100, St Margaret's 200, St Giles (Gilesgate) 60, St Mary's, North Bailey 60 and 24 died in the jail. The Bishop of Durham Tobias Matthew has retired to his castle at Stockton as a place of refuge.

## 1598
### PLAGUE CONTINUES
The plague ceased at Durham at the beginning of the year but broke out again in September.

## 1601
### FIRST MAYOR
Durham City has received a charter of incorporation from the crown but Bishop Tobias Matthew has objected to this as an infringement of his rights and the charter has been quoshed. The bishop has instead granted a charter himself and has appointed Hugh Wright as the first mayor of Durham. Durham City will be administered by the Mayor, 12 alderman and 24 burgesses.

## April 13th 1603
### KING JAMES VISITS DURHAM
James VI King of Scotland newly appointed as James I King of England has visited Durham during his long journey south to claim the Crown of England. King James has been entertained in the castle by the Bishop of Durham, who attended him with a hundred gentlemen.

## 1604
### PLAGUE IN GILESGATE
The last recorded incidence of the plague in Durham broke out in St Giles parish, Gilesgate Durham this year.

## 1615
### SPENNYMOOR MUSTER
An assembly of men between the age of 16 and 60 fit to bear arms in the county of Durham gathered at Spenny Moor near Whitworth. The total number of men was 8,320 of which 560 came from the city and suburbs of Durham.

# Elvet Old & New

*April 1617*

**MAYOR GREETS KING**

*King James I has visited Durham during a journey into Scotland. Entering by Elvet the King was greeted by a loyal speech from the mayor of Durham on horseback. The mayor, bearing the city mace rode before the king in a great procession to the cathedral.*

*1617*

**MARKET CROSS ERECTED**

*A market cross has been erected in Durham. Covered with lead, it consists of twelve stone pillars.*

*August 18th 1618*

**HORSE THIEF EXECUTED**

*A horse thief by the name of Thomas Wright has been executed at Dryburn, Durham. He has been burried at St Oswald's Church, in Elvet.*

*March 1633*

**MAN PUNISHED FOR CLANDESTINE MARRIAGE**

*A man has had to make a public penitential confession in Durham and ordered to pay a £40 fine for a clandestine marriage performed by a Roman Catholic priest in a private house in Crossgate, Durham City.*

*June 1st 1633*

**FOOL ENTERTAINS KING**

*King Charles I stayed three days in Durham while on his way to Scotland. During his stay at Durham Castle, the King was attended by the Earls of Newcastle, Northumberland and Pembroke and amused by Dickie Pearson, the Bishop of Durham's fool. The Earl of Pembroke was very elaborately and fantastically dressed which prompted Dickie to ask in a very familiar manner 'I am the Bishop of Durham's fool, whose fool are you?'. The Bishop of Durham's cost for entertaining the king amounted to £1,500 per day.*

*August 27th 1637*

**STEEPLE FALLS INTO STREET**

*The steeple of St Mary le Bow Church in the Bailey Durham collapsed into the street today, a large part of the western church was brought down but nobody was injured.*

## THE SWAN'S ISLAND

Elvet across the River Wear to the east of the Durham peninsula is bounded by the river on its western, northern and eastern sides so that like the 'Dun Holm' it forms an 'island', although considerably· flatter in appearance. Records of Elvet's existence predate the settlement of Dunholm in 995 A.D so it may have been a place of importance.

Anciently Elvet was called Aelfet- ee which in a very old tongue meant 'Swan Island'. This is recorded in 'The Anglo-Saxon Chronicle' as the place where a certain Peotwine was consecrated as the Bishop of Whithorn in the year 762 A.D. The consecration took place two hundred and thirty three years before the foundation of Durham in 995 A.D. At the time the Durham peninsula is thought to have been a densely wooded uninhabitable area. Elvet, flatter and more accessible may have been settled and cultivated.

It is worth noting that Simeon of Durham, an eleventh century historian with access to ancient documents, suggested the existence of an earlier settlement in the vicinity of Durham. He describes a small cultivated plain which was regularly ploughed and sown by farmers before the settlement of St Cuthbert's carriers in 995 A.D. Perhaps the farmers lived on a small agricultural settlement at Elvet.

## PUDSEY'S BRIDGE

The first mention of Elvet in Norman times was during the episcopacy of Bishop William St Carileph who granted the area to the Prior and Convent of Durham as a free borough 'with licence to maintain forty merchant's houses free from secular service'. Elvet was seemingly a suburb of considerable size. In the twelfth century during the time of Bishop Pudsey (1153-1195) the growth of the borough of Elvet was further stimulated by the construction of Elvet Bridge linking Elvet to Saddler Street on the Durham peninsula. Repairs were carried out around 1500 by Bishop Fox and in 1771 further reconstructions were undertaken after three arches were destroyed in a great flood that wrecked most of the bridges on the Wear, Tyne and Tees.

*Elvet Bridge in the January snows of 1970*

Elvet Bridge has seven arches of which three are dry 'land arches' Two of the arches are hidden by buildings. In medieval times a number of buildings were situated upon this bridge including two chapels which stood at either end.

One building still exists on the bridge today above a dry arch and can be identified by its Dutch Gabled exterior. It is situated at the Elvet end of the bridge on the site of the medieval Chapel of St Andrew.

# GHOST OF A GYPSY PIPER

At the Saddler Street end of Elvet Bridge stood St James's Chapel which was replaced by a House of Correction in 1632. Two prison cells associated with the House of Correction can be seen beneath the western land arch of Elvet Bridge. The cells are reputed to be haunted by the ghost of Jimmy Allan, a gypsy piper who was one of the most notorious and colourful characters in the history of Northumbria.

Jimmy was an adopted member of the Faas, a famous gypsy clan who inhabited the Cheviot Hills near Kirk Yetholm on the border between England and Scotland. Jimmy's father Wull Faa,

## April 1639
### KING CHARLES VISIT
*King Charles I has visited Durham while on his way north to march against the Scottish Covenanters. He has been entertained by Morton, the Bishop of Durham during his stay. The king then proceeded to Berwick where he made temporary peace with the Scots deputies.*

## August 30th 1640
### SCOTS SEIZE DURHAM
*An English army was heavily defeated by Scottish covenanters at the Battle of Newburn on Tyne on August 28. Newcastle has been fully occupied by the Scots who have also seized the City and Castle of Durham which had been a Royalist stronghold.*

## 1641
### SCOTS LEAVE DURHAM
*The Scots have disbanded from their occupation of Durham and other parts of the north after receiving £60,000 from King Charles.*

## 1646
### CROMWELL ABOLISHES BISHOP'S REVENUE
*Parliament has abolished the episcopy of Durham. The revenues of the see have been taken from the Bishop of Durham by Oliver Cromwell's House of Commons.*

## 1649
### LONDON LORD MAYOR BUYS DURHAM CASTLE
*Durham Castle, formerly the home of the now powerless Bishop of Durham has been bought by Thomas Andrews the Lord Mayor of London for £1267 10d. He has greatly defaced the property and made it virtually uninhabitable.*

## March 1650
### CROMWELL PROPOSES COLLEGE FOR DURHAM
*Oliver Cromwell has suggested that the siting of a college at Durham would be 'a matter of great concernment and importance which may conduce to the promoting of learning and piety in these rude and ignorant partes'*

## April 18th 1650
### FRAMWELLGATE SOLD TO CORPORATION
*Framwellgate and the Borough of Durham, which formerly belonged to the Bishopric of Durham, have been sold to the Corporation of Durham for £200.*

## July 14th 1650
### CROMWELL VISITS DURHAM
*Oliver Cromwell has visited the City of Durham today prior to the Battle of Dunbar. (He stayed in a house which is now part of the Royal County Hotel in Old Elvet.)*

## September 1650
### SCOTS PRISONERS WRECK CATHEDRAL
*Following the defeat of the Scots at the Battle of Dunbar, over three thousand Scottish captives have been imprisoned in Durham Cathedral. Many fine tombs have been destroyed by the prisoners and ancient woodwork has been destroyed for firewood. Only an ornamented clock featuring the sacred Scottish thistle seems to have been spared.*

## January 1652
### WITCHCRAFT EXECUTIONS
*Two men by the name of Adamson and Powle have been executed in the City of Durham for witchcraft.*

## May 15th 1657
### UNIVERSITY QUOSHED BY OXBRIDGE
*Oliver Cromwell has signed a writ of privy seal for the establishment of a University at Durham. The writ has been suppressed due to pressure from the Universities of Oxford and Cambridge who have objected to the proposals.*

## November 2nd 1660
### BISHOPRIC RESTORED
*The restoration of King Charles II to the English throne has been heartily celebrated in Durham City. The County Palatine and Bishopric of Durham have been restored to Bishop John Cosin who has begun the restoration of his castle at Durham which was severely defaced during its ownership by the Lord Mayor of London.*

*House of Correction, Elvet Bridge*

'The Gypsy King' had taught him to play the Northumbrian pipes at a very young age and the young man's musical talents caught the attention of people far and wide until he eventually succeeded in becoming the official piper to the Duchess of Northumberland, a post he held for two years.

Unfortunately Jimmy was a man of many diversions with a great love of drinking and gambling and an eye for pretty women, many of whom he conned out of purse. Cattle stealing was another of Jimmy's vices but his favourite pastime seems to have been enlisting and deserting from British and Foreign armies.

On the run for most of his life, Jimmy was pursued far and wide for desertion and other crimes. He was locked up twice and escaped twice, running off to Edinburgh and Dublin where he astonished the residents of those cities with his musical abilities. His journeys took him much further still to the Dutch East Indies via India and to the Baltic 'without any passport but his pipes'.

In 1803 Jimmy was finally arrested at Jedburgh in the borders for stealing a horse from Gateshead in the County of Durham. From Jedburgh he was taken to Durham where he was tried and sentenced to death. Luckily for him someone intervened and his sentence was reduced to life imprisonment .

Jimmy remained locked up in the cell beneath Durham's Elvet Bridge for seven years where he eventually died in the year 1810 aged seventy seven. He was rather unfortunate because a pardon had been granted which arrived only a few days after his death. As for the cells underneath Elvet Bridge, it is said that if you listen carefully you may still be able to hear the eerie, haunting musical sounds of Jimmy's Northumbrian pipes - it is Jimmy's ghost of course!

## OLD ELVET

Elvet Bridge leads directly from Saddler Street on the peninsula into the wide street called Old Elvet which was once the site of the city's horse fair. Many of the buildings in Old Elvet are of eighteenth century origin with one of the obvious exceptions being the imposing Old Shire Hall, a Victorian red brick building topped with a green copper dome.

The Old Shire Hall, built in 1895 (extended in 1909) was originally the County Hall for Durham before it was replaced by the modern County Hall to the north of the city in the 1960s. Since 1963 the Shire Hall has been the administrative headquarters of the University of Durham.

Historically the hall has an important place in the history of the British Labour party as it was here in 1909 that the first all Labour County Council in Britain assembled. The first chairman of this council was Mr Peter Lee (1864-1935) a former miner's leader who had started his

*Old Elvet looking towards Elvet Bridge at the turn of the century. (Durham City Reference Library)*

### June 21st 1675
**MP DIES FOUR DAYS AFTER ELECTION**
*John Tempest, with 1034 votes and Thomas Vane of Raby Castle with 856 votes were elected as Durham County's first Members of Parliament. Thomas Vane, died of smallpox four days after his election and has been suceeded by his younger brother Christopher Vane.*

### March 27th 1678
**CITY ELECTS FIRST MPS**
*Sir Ralph Cole of Brancepeth Castle, with 408 votes and John Parkhurst of Catesby, Northampton, 379 votes have been elected as the first parliamentary representatives for Durham City.*

### 1680
**MAYOR IS A DUCK**
*John Duck, known as Durham's Dick Whittington has become mayor of Durham.*

### 1680
**DEAN STARTS COLLECTION**
*Dean Sudbury of Durham has set up a new library for the Dean and Chapter of Durham. The library will become a place for the deposit of Roman inscriptions found in the north and many ancient manuscripts including works by Bede.*

### April 26th 1682
**FLOOD HITS DURHAM**
*There has been a great flood in the River Wear at Durham.*

### April 1683
**DURHAM RACES**
*In this year there has been the first recorded incidence of racing in Durham.*

### September 15th 1683
**GLAZIER PILLORIED**
*A glazier from Gateshead by the name of Simpson has had to stand for an hour and a half in the pilory at Durham for accepting a bribe from a Quaker.*

working life at Littletown colliery to the west of Durham City at the age of only ten. Today Peter Lee is commemorated in the name of Peterlee New Town in the eastern part of County Durham.

The other prominent building in Old Elvet after the Shire Hall is the Royal County Hotel, created from four existing buildings in the 1970s one of which was already known as the Royal County. Further extensions have been made recently but many parts of the building date from the eighteenth century and earlier. The exterior of the hotel is noted for its balcony on which prominent members of the Labour party view the passing crowds on Miners' Gala Day. Inside, the hotel is notable for its impressive staircase dating from 1660. It is said to have been brought from Loch Leven Castle.

## THE BIG MEETING

Old Elvet leads towards the riverside sports grounds on the area of land once known as the Smiddy Haughs, which means the smooth meadow or smith's meadow. This is commonly known as the 'Racecourse' though races have not been held here for many decades. Dating from at least the seventeenth century, the Durham race meetings were very popular with people from throughout the region and on April 14, 1873 a crowd of 80,000 people attended. The crowd stunned the people of Durham and brought the little city to a stand still. To add to the problem

## September 28th 1684

**BISHOP REFUSES BURIAL**

*A tanner from Framwellgate by the name of John Richardson has been refused burial at Crossgate Church by the Bishop because he was under sentence of excommunication. The man has been buried in his garden at Caterhouse.*

## 1685

**NEW CHARTER FAILS**

*A new charter for the city of Durham has been introduced by Nathaniel, Lord Crewe, the Bishop of Durham. The charter will however be quoshed because of an error and the 1602 charter will remain in force.*

## January 4th 1688

**OLDEST RESIDENT DIES**

*An old lady by the name of Mrs Hutchinson has died in Durham City aged 103 years.*

## January 16th 1691

**DUCK DIES**

*John Duck, the former Mayor of Durham known as Durham's Dick Whittington has died today.*

## April 23rd 1699

**FIVE INCH HAIL FALLS ON DURHAM**

*Hail stones measuring five inches in diameter have fallen upon Durham and its surroundings today.*

## January 15th 1711

**CHRONOLOGIST DIES**

*Mr Jacob Bee, author of the Bee Diaries, a record of unusual events and occurences has died. Durham born Bee, a former skinner and glover has been buried at St Margaret's Durham. In his later years Bee had been an outpensioner of Sherburn Hospital.*

## 1718

**SCHOOL FOUNDED**

*The Blue-Coat School has been founded in Durham City.*

a second meeting was to be held the next day and there was a desperate shortage of accomodation so that many of the townsfolk offered their homes as lodgings for the night.

This crowd may have been great, but in later years it was completely eclipsed by the massive attendances at the Durham Miners' Gala which was also held on the Racecourse. Traditionally held on the third Saturday in July, the Miners' Gala or 'Big Meeting' could in its heyday attract up to 300,000 people, which is remarkable when we consider that the present population of County Durham is less than 600,000. The streets of the city thronged with people as large crowds of representatives and residents from each colliery village marched towards the racecourse accompanied by their brass bands to hear the speeches of the Labour leaders. The contingents from each colliery could be easily identified by their unique colliery lodge banners many of which were considered works of art.

## THROW HIM IN THE RIVER

The miners who flocked to the gala (pronounced Gayla) went to demonstrate their unity and claim their rights to a fair pay and safe working conditions. These men had little sympathy for those with right wing views and this was demonstrated by an amusing incident which occured at the gala in 1925.

In that year unemployment was particularly high in the County Durham coalfield at a time when a certain Hensley Henson was Bishop of Durham. Henson became bishop in 1920 during a miners' strike and strongly criticised the use of strike action. This won Henson few friends among the miners and at the gala of 1925 when a group of miners thought they spotted the Bishop, he was lifted from his feet and escorted to the river where it is said they attempted to throw him in. Fortunately the man fell into a boat, losing his hat and umbrella in the process. Lucky for him, because it turned out that this was not the Bishop at all but the Dean of Durham, Dr J Weldon, who was at the gala to give a speech about the evils of drink!

## BEHIND BARS

One of Durham's best known buildings is of course the prison which was built at Elvet in 1810 to replace the earlier jail situated in the now long since destroyed Great North Gate. The new prison was constructed with the assistance of Bishop Shute Barrington who was keen to see the destruction of the old jail which caused a great inconvenience to traffic. Barrington pledged £2000 towards the construction of the new building and on 31 July 1809 the foundation stones were laid by Sir Henry Vane Tempest.

The building was initially constructed by a Mr Sandys who also built the nearby courts but his work was criticised and he was dismissed before its completion. Most of the work of Sandys was removed and a new architect was employed by the name of Moneypenny but he died during its construction and the work was completed by the famous Durham architect Ignatius Bonomi.

The prisoners were not transferred to the Elvet prison until 1819 but an execution of a murderer by the name of John Grieg took place here in 1816. Conditions in the new jail were probably better than those in the Great North Gate but it is interesting to note that in 1827 the pris-

*Durham Jail*

oner diet was confined to two helpings of oatmeal porridge and a pound of bread on Mondays, Wednesdays and Saturdays. On other days they were treated to potatoes and fish.

Durham prison has about 600 cells and at least one ghost who reputedly haunts a cell on the ground floor of the main wing which had to be converted into a storeroom following complaints from prisoners who claimed to witness a ghostly murder in the cell during the night. It is said that a former occupant of the cell was stabbed to death by another inmate.

## 'NEE GUD LUCK IN DURHAM JAIL'

Durham Jail has been the long term home to many notorious criminals and a short term home to many lesser offenders like Tommy Armstrong (1848-1919), a bow-legged miner from Tanfield Lea who was known· as the 'Pitman Poet' because of his talent for composing songs about life in the Durham coalfield.

Tommy had a fondness for the drink and it was during a period of drunkenness that the incident occured which resulted in his imprisonment at Durham. According to his plea he had stumbled into the Co-Operative store in the town of Stanley and pinched a pair of stockings which had a bow legged appearance that would have fitted him perfectly.

### 1720
**MUSTARD MADE**
*In this year the world's first commercial production of mustard has begun in Durham City by a Mrs Clements whose secret recipe has become very popular throughout the country.*

### 1720
**PLAN TO LINK TYNE AND WEAR BY CANAL**
*A plan has been been put forward to join the River Tyne and Wear via a canal adjoining the River Team.*

### July 8th 1721
**WEAR RISES**
*The River Wear rose to a very great height in Durham City today.*

### 1725
**CHOCOLATE POISONERS TO BE WHIPPED**
*John Brown and Christopher Richardson of Gateshead have been sentenced to imprisonment today for attempting to poison their master William Coatsworth by putting arsenic into his chocolate. It has been ordered that they are to be annually whipped ten times in the market place for the duration of their sentence on the tenth day of June, being the anniversary of their crime.*

### August 20th 1725
**MURDERER EXECUTED**
*Thomas Charlton, a murderer, bigamist and robber from North Tynedale, Northumberland has been executed in Durham today for the brutal killing of his illegal wife.*

### June 7th 1727
**DURHAM UNDER FLOOD**
*A great flood has hit Durham and completely blocked off all communication between Durham and the nearby village of Shincliffe for nearly twelve hours.*

### June 21st 1727
**SECOND FLOOD IN MONTH HITS DURHAM**
*Yet another flood has innundated Durham, this is the second major flood this month.*

## 1727
### MAN HANGED FOR MURDER OF PREGNANT WOMAN
*Mr William Stephenson, a grocer from Northallerton was hanged at Durham today for the murder of Mary Farding who was pregnant by him. Mr Stephenson had thrown Miss Farding into the sea at Hartlepool.*

## 1729
### NEPTUNE BROUGHT TO MARKET PLACE
*A statue of Neptune, God of the Oceans has been erected in the Market Square Durham. The statue covering the octagon fountain was presented by George Bowes and is symbolic of Durham's aspirations to be a sea port.*

## August 1732
### THIEF BAPTISED AND EXECUTED
*Two notorious horse thiefs, John and James Graham were executed at Durham today. James Graham chose to be baptised at St Mary le Bow Church in the Bailey, on the morning of his execution.*

## February 19th 1737
### PRISONERS ESCAPE
*Two prisoners have escaped from Durham Jail in Saddler Street. The prisoners, John Dodsworth and John Penman escaped from the jail at around ten o' clock at night after viciously knocking down the under keeper of the prison.*

## 1740
### PLAN TO MAKE DURHAM A SEA PORT
*A new plan has been put forward to make the River Wear navigable from the sea to Durham City. This would greatly increase the trade and merchant wealth of Durham if it became an inland sea port.*

During his time in prison Tommy Armstrong composed one of his best known songs. Entitled 'Nee Gud Luck in Dorham Jail', it gives an unusual insight into life in the prison. Here are some of the verses:

*Durham Jail by Thomas Armstrong (1848-1919)*

*Ye'l awl hev ard o' Dorham Jail, But it wad ye much sorprise, To see the prisoners in the yard, When they're on exorcise The yard is built eroond wi' walls, Se' noabil and se' strang, Whe ivor gans there heh te' bide thor time, be it short or lang*

*CHORUS: There's nee gud luck in Dorham Jail There's nee gud luck at awl Whats the breed en skilly for But just te' make ye small*

*When ye gan te' Dorham Jail They'll find ye wi emploi, They'll dress ye up se dandy In a suit o cordy roy; They'll fetch a cap wi'oot a peak, En nivvor axe yer size En like yer suite its cordy roy En cums doon ower yer eyes*

*The Forst month is th' worst of aal Yor feelins' they will try There's nowt but two greet lumps e' wood, On which ye hae to lie Then eftor that ye gans te' bed, But it is ard as stoanes It neet ye daresn't make a torn In case ye break some bones*

Tommy's song finishes with a spoken passage about life in the Jail:

*That's the place te gan if yer matched te fight; Thorl fetch ye doon te yor weight if yer ower heavy. They feed ye on the floor broth ivory meal en thee put it doon at the front for e' th' hoose yer livin' in. When the tornkey opens the door, upt yer hand oot an ye'l get a had iv a shot box we bee lid, an vary little inside it; its grand stuff for the women folks te paper their wall with. It sticks te yor ribs, but its not made for a man that hes te hew coals. Bide away if they'll let ye.*

# NEW ELVET, KINGSGATE & HALLGARTH STREET

The street of New Elvet joins Old Elvet from the west and until the 1930s when new buildings were constructed it was of a very similar appearance to Old Elvet. Today the most imposing buildings are the concrete Dunelm House which is Durham University's Student Union building (1961-65), and the Three Tuns Hotel.

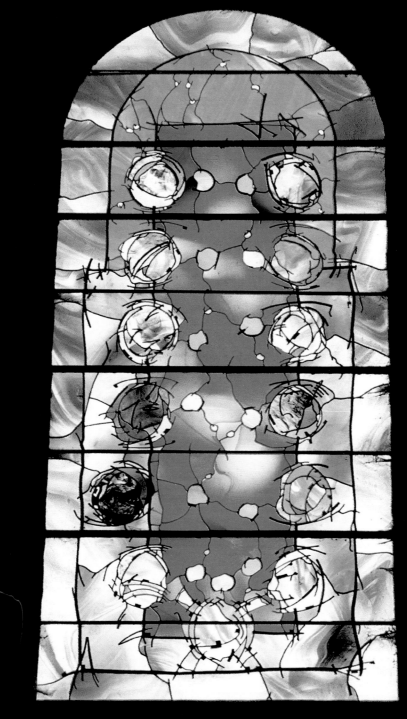

The Daily Bread Window at Durham Cathedral donated by staff at Marks & Spencers, Durham in celebration of the firms centenary in 1984.
Designed by Mark Angus

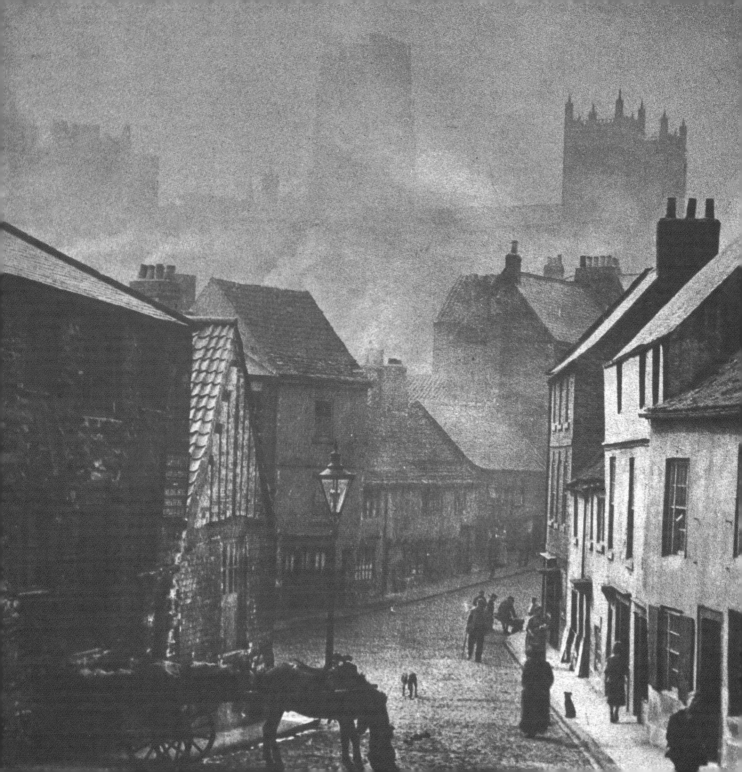

Above: The Fram Well from which Framwellgate gets its name.

Opposite: The ancient streets of Framwellgate and Millburngate at the beginning of the century. All the houses in this picture have now gone.

## A Central Tower

The original Central Tower or Belfry Tower was struck by lightning in 1429 and replaced in the same century. In 1346 during the Battle of Neville's Cross, a group of monks cheered the English to victory from the top of the tower.

## B Prior's Kitchen

The distinctive octagonal outline of the Priory kitchen is one of the most distinctive architectural features of Durham's monastic buildings.

## C Saint Cuthbert's Feretory

Saint Cuthbert's tomb lies in this elevated feretory behind the Neville Screen. At one time this was the most easterly point of the cathedral before the building of the neighbouring Chapel of the Nine Altars in the thirteenth century. The original eastern outline of the cathedral, in the shape of an apse is marked on the floor.

## D Font & font cover

This prominent font was built during the episcopal reign of the seventeenth century Bishop John Cosin.

## E Cuthbert of Farne

Carving of St Cuthbert placed in the Cloister Garth in 1981.

The carving was made by Fenwick Lawson from a famous elm tree which stood outside the north door of the cathedral.

## F Marble marker

In monastic times women were not allowed to cross this marble marker and were confined to the Galilee Chapel. This Benedictine rule may have reinforced the legend that St Cuthbert disliked women.

## G Galilee Chapel

Constructed around 1174 by Bishop Hugh Pudsey, the Galilee Chapel or Lady Chapel was once the only part of the cathedral women were allowed to enter.

## H Tomb of the Venerable Bede

The bones of Bede were brought to Durham in 1022 when they were acquired from the ruined monastery of Jarrow by a relic collector.
Bede's tomb is inscribed with a Latin poem.

## Cloister Walkway

The buildings surrounding the Cloister Garth were formerly the monastic buildings of Durham Priory. On the eastern side of the cloisters is the Chapter House, accessible from a door beneath the cathedral clock, but not open to the public. The Chapter House contains the tombs of Bishops Pudsey, Flambard and St Carileph.

*Mason's Mark* (background picture) A distinctive mark left by an anonymous mason employed in the building of Durham Cathedral.

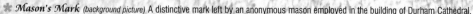

# Nine Centuries of Durham Cathedral

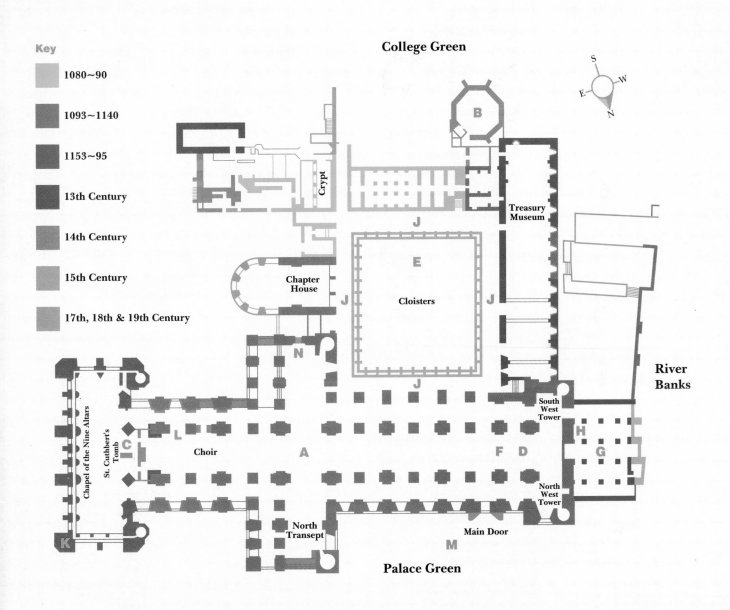

**College Green**

**Key**

- 1080~90
- 1093~1140
- 1153~95
- 13th Century
- 14th Century
- 15th Century
- 17th, 18th & 19th Century

**Treasury Museum**

Crypt

J

E

Cloisters

J

J

J

B

Chapter House

N

South West Tower

**River Banks**

Chapel of the Nine Altars

St. Cuthbert's Tomb

C

L

Choir

A

F

D

H

G

K

North Transept

Main Door

M

North West Tower

**Palace Green**

World Cross Country Championships at Maiden Castle, Durham 1995

Dop: Ian Botham playing for Durham C.C.C.

Durham Wasps celebrate another victory

Durham Regatta

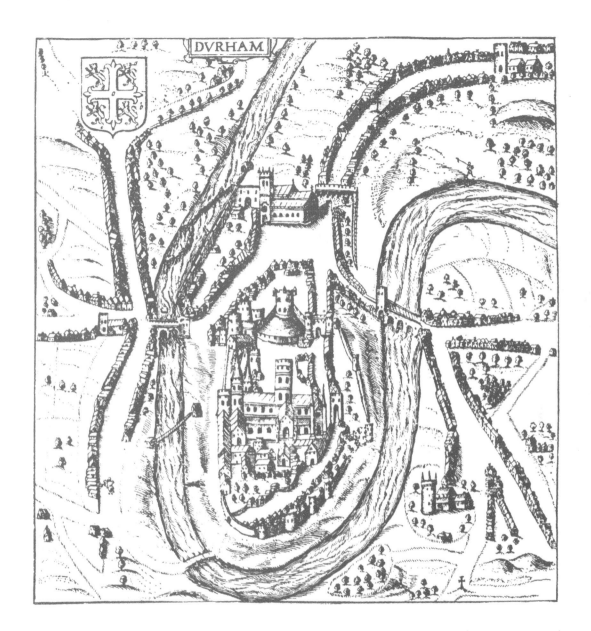

Speed's map of Durham City, 1610

### K Pinnacle

During 1995 this north eastern pinnacle of the Chapel of the Nine altars was undergoing repair. Ancient buildings like Durham Cathedral are in constant need of restoration.

### L Bishop's Tomb (seen below)

The tomb of the fourteenth century Bishop Thomas Hatfield lies beneath the Bishop of Durham's 'Cathedra' or throne. This throne is the highest in Christendom, in keeping with the once mighty status of Durham's Prince Bishops.

### M Tightrope Walker's Tomb

This tomb outside the North Door is reputedly the grave of a tightrope walker who fell to his death in 1237 while attempting to walk a tightrope attached to the towers of the cathedral.

### N Cathedral Clock

The sixteenth century decorated Cathedral Clock was the only woodwork not used as firewood by the four thousand Scottish prisoners locked up in the cathedral after the Battle of Dunbar in 1650. It is said the Scots were reluctant to burn the clock because it included a carving of their sacred Scottish thistle. More importantly it helped them tell the time.

In days gone the Three Tuns was noted for Mrs Brown's cherry brandy which was presented with the compliments of the landlady to any traveller who resided here for the night. This was an old English custom which is said to have survived at the Three Tuns longer than anywhere else along the Great North Road.

Other notable houses of refreshment in the vicinity include the Swan and Three Cygnets, the name of which reminds us that Elvet means 'Swan Island'. On the opposite side of the bridge we can see an historic house built on the dry arch of Elvet Bridge

At Dunelm House New Elvet splits into two streets called Hallgarth Street and Church Street near the latter of which a lane leads the walker across the River Wear via Kingsgate Footbridge. Used mainly by students the bridge was built by the great Civil Engineer Ove Arup (1895-1988). Arup was responsible for many great projects including the Sydney Opera House but he always considered the Kingsgate Bridge his favourite work. The bridge dates from 1963 and is built of Shap granite aggregate.

The road on the left fork from New Elvet signposted to Stockton is Hallgarth Street. It takes its name from the site of a hall belonging to the priors of Durham called Hallgarth. Associated with the hall was Hallgarth Tithe Barn a medieval structure which can still be seen. It was used to house the portion of the local harvest which the prior's tenants owed to the monastery of Durham

# OSWALD'S CHURCH

Church Street, adjoining New Elvet takes its name from the nearby Church of St Oswald. The earliest part of this church dates from the twelfth century but the site is thought to be older as a number of Anglo Saxon finds have been discovered. The finds included five pre-conquest sculptures incorporated into the wall of the church which were removed in the later part of the nineteenth century.

---

## September 1745
### MUSTER ON THE MOOR
*A muster of one thousand men from the county of Durham has gathered on Framwellgate Moor in a show of loyalty to the king at a time when the Jacobite supporters of Bonnie Prince Charlie and the rebellion in Scotland are considered a threat.*

## October 1745
### DURHAM PREPARES FOR REBELLION
*One thousand horse have been quartered at Durham in preparation for an onslaught by Scottish rebels. There are huge numbers of English troops stationed at Berwick and Newcastle.*

## November 5th 1745
### TROOPS CELEBRATE GUY FAWKES ANNIVERSARY
*Troops mustered in the fields around Durham fired three vollies in celebration of the Gunpowder Plot before entering the city to celebrate the event in the Rose and Crown in Silver Street.*

## January 27th 1746
### PRINCE WELCOMED
*His Royal Highness the Duke of Cumberland was welcomed into Durham at eight o'clock this evening. The Duke was greeted by the mayor, recorder and alderman and marched in a great procession through the illuminated city. Thousands of people watched the spectacle and gave great cheer.*

## September 8th 1746
### FOUR ESCAPE FROM JAIL
*Three men and one woman have escaped from Durham Jail with their irons still on.*

## August 15th 1748
### HIGHWAYMAN EXECUTED
*A Highwayman from London who had taken up lodgings in Newcastle was executed today for robbing two men at Durham City and Elvet Moor. The victims were a Mr Colling and Mr Hutchinson, a Durham City attorney, whose watch was taken. The highwayman, Paul Coleman, took Mr Hutchinson's horse which he used to make his way back to Newcastle. Gunpowder, slugs and flints were later found at Coleman's lodgings.*

**August 27th 1750**
**MAN EXECUTED FOR
ROBBING 10 YEAR OLD**
*James MacFidum was executed in Durham today
for robbing a ten year old boy on his way to school
at Whickham near Gateshead last year.*

**February 17th 1753**
**FLOOD DESTROYS BRIDGE**
*Two arches of Shincliffe Bridge near Durham were
carried away by the rising River Wear today.*

**May 13th 1758**
**REGIMENT FORMED**
*The 68th regiment of foot soldiers under the charge
of John Lambton has formed. This is the forerunner
of what will later become the Durham Light Infantry*

**July 13th 1759**
**FREEDOM FOR RIVER MEN**
*Richard, Earl of Scarborough, Richard Trevor,
Bishop of Durham and the Honourable James
Lumley have been presented with the freedom of
the city by the corporation of Durham. They have
been awarded for promoting the navigation of the
River Wear. This year parliament gave the go ahead
for the river improvement, although little work
seems to have been carried out.*

**1760**
**BRIDGE BUILDINGS REMOVED**
*A historic gateway tower has been removed from
the end of Framwellgate Bridge because it has
proved to be an obstruction for carriages. A
number of crowded buildings have also been
removed from the north pillars of Elvet Bridge.*

*Elvet Bridge*

Studies show that the sculptures may date from some time before the settlement on the peninsula of Durham called Dun Holm. It therefore seems likely that this area was the place where Bishop Peotwine was consecrated in 762 A.D.

The fact that the church is dedicated to St Oswald may also be of signifcance as this is the only ancient church in Northumberland or Durham dedicated to him. St Oswald was in fact a king of Northumbria (634-641 A.D) who converted the people of his kingdom to Christianity with the assistance of St Aidan, a predecessor of St Cuthbert. It seems possible that Elvet may have been a place of importance in King Oswald's time.

In the churchyard across the road from St Oswald's we find the grave of Dr John Bacchus Dykes, founder of Cambridge University Musical Society. Principally famous for composing the hymn tunes for 'Jesu Lover of My Soul' and 'Nearer my God to thee'. He was the Vicar at St Oswalds from 1864 until his death in 1876

## MOUNT JOY AND MAIDEN CASTLE

From New Elvet Hallgarth Street leads out of the city by the A177 (the Shincliffe Peth) into the surrounding countryside. The road leads past two very historic sites which lie just beyond the outskirts of Elvet on either side of the road. To the west is the small hill called Mount Joy near Houghall wood and on a hill to the east is the site of Maiden Castle which is completely surrounded by an old oak woodland.

Mount Joy is of course the place associated with the legend of the Dun Cow and the carriers of St Cuthbert's coffin in 995 A.D but its name may also be connected with an old French term. In France Mont Joie was the place where pilgrims heaped stones when they gained sight of the end of a pilgrimage. Mount Joy, Durham was perhaps the place where Norman pilgrims to the shrine of St Cuthbert carried out a similar practice.

The promontory fort of Maiden Castle has never been properly examined but may be an Iron Age fortress belonging to the ancient British tribe called the Brigantes who were strongly associated with North Yorkshire and County Durham. The name Maiden Castle does seem to originate from Ancient British times and may derive from Moe Din, Moe meaning grassy plain Din meaning fort. Alternatively it could mean a 'virgin' fought' which has not had to fight a battle. There are a number of other Maiden Castles in England including a gigantic promontory fort in Dorset and a smaller example near Reeth in the northern part of Yorkshire.

Another suggestion regarding the origin of Maiden Castle is that it is the site of an ancient fortress called Caer Weir . This is referred to by Welsh chroniclers as a place held by the Anglo-Saxons during their early battles against King Arthur and the Welsh speaking Britons who once inhabited the north.

In reality the exact origins of Maiden Castle are unknown but its situation on a hill called Maiden Scaur or Nab End would certainly have provided good protection from attack. This is particularly so on the eastern side where there is a steep climb up the escarpment near the River Wear.

It is perhaps not as well defended as it may have been in Iron Age times as by natural processes the River Wear which afforded it extra protection has gradually moved its course away from the site. There is very little to be seen of the ancient fort of Maiden Castle today as over the years the traces of its rampart ditch have slowly eroded away.

# Gilesgate & Old Durham

## OLD DURHAM

Directly across the eastern side of the river from Elvet and the ancient Maiden Castle is Old Durham in the vicinity of Gilesgate. This area could once be reached from the Elvet side of the river by a ford which crossed the river from Green Lane near the old race course. Anciently the area may have had strong links with Maiden Castle as Old Durham was a Roman site. This in turn may have had connections with a possible third ancient site in the nearby Pelaw Wood. Pelaw is said to derive its name from Pele Law meaning 'Fort Hill'.

It was known for many years that a Roman Road ran somewhere in the vicinity of Durham. Called 'Cade's Road', its course can be traced from Shincliffe to the River Tees in the south and between Chester le Street and Newcastle in the north. In the immediate area of Durham the course of the road has been lost without trace.

In 1974 excavations beneath the cathedral cloister uncovered some Roman pottery and a Roman coin which may indicate the site of a native Roman-British farm on the peninsula, that is a native farm which came under a slight degree of Roman influence. It seems unlikely however that the largely inaccessible peninsula accomodated the site of a Roman Road

Old Durham near Gilesgate had long been suggested as the site of a Roman settlement and this theory seemed to be reinforced during a hot dry Summer in the last century when the remains of old bridge piers were exposed in the River Wear at Old Durham and further north at Kepier. It was suggested that these were the two points at which the old Roman Road crossed the River Wear on its way north towards Hadrian's Wall.

The probability of a Roman Road here became more likely when in 1940 an accidental find during quarrying at Old Durham led to the discovery of the site of a Roman Bath House. Once capable of producing both dry and damp heat, the bath house is believed to have been associated with an adjacent Roman villa - the northernmost in the Roman Empire. Excavations at Old Durham suggest that the site was occupied from the second century to the fourth century A.D. There is nothing to be seen of the site today.

Old Durham was the site of a seventeenth century mansion belonging to the Heath family. This mansion was demolished in the following century but its terraced gardens still remain. Throughout the last century and into the present century Old Durham, its gardens and a nearby pub called the Pineapple Inn were a very popular place of recreation for people who came from miles around. Older residents of the city can recall Summer picnics outside the pub.

### 1761
**BYLAW MAKES NEW FREEMEN**
*A bylaw has been introduced by the corporation of Durham which creates new freemen who are entitled to vote for the election of MPs in the city.*

### May 11th 1762
**MP DISPUTE SETTLED BY PARLIAMENT**
*The outcome of the parliamentary election in Durham last December has been successfully disputed by the losing candidate, Major General John Lambton. Major General Lambton claimed that the outcome of the election was determined by the votes of the occasional freeman and that if their votes had been set aside he would have been victorious by 192 votes. Today the House of Commons resolved that the occasional freemen had no right to vote and that the present MP Ralph Gowland must step down in General Lambton's favour. On entering the city of Durham, as new MP, the General was greeted by celebration*

### January 18th 1763
**SKATING ON THE RIVER**
*The River Wear has frozen over at Durham and prompted many of the inhabitants of the city to indulge in the passtime of skating.*

### Oct 6th 1765
**OLDEST RESIDENT DIES**
*Margaret Green, Durham's oldest resident died today aged 102. She is said to have retained her senses until the very end.*

### September 1768
**SHOP FALLS INTO RIVER**
*The floor of a smith's shop on Elvet Bridge collapsed just as the smith opened the door to enter it. All his tools plunged into the river, and were followed shortly after by the whole fabric of the building itself.*

### 1769
**MOOR DIVIDED UP**
*The two hundred acre Crossgate Moor near Durham has been divided up. The Dean and Chapter will reserve six pence per acre and revenue from mining.*

## November 8th 1770
### FLOODING IN THE CITY
*The River Wear has flooded Durham City today and several cellars in the neighbourhood of Elvet have overflowed causing great damage.*

## July 10th 1771
### NEW THEATRE
*A new theatre was opened on the north side of Drury Lane off Saddler Street, today with a performance of 'The West Indian'. The theatre replaces an earlier theatre which stood a little further down Drury Lane.*

## November 1771
### BIGGEST FLOOD EVER HITS DURHAM
*A great river flood has hit the north destroying several bridges and claiming lives on the Tyne and Tees. The River Wear at Durham is eight feet ten inches higher than ever before. At the end of Framwellgate Bridge two houses have been swept away, a water mill belonging to the cathedral has been severely damaged and a bridge belonging to the Dean and Chapter has been completely destroyed. Four of the arches of Elvet Bridge have been carried away by the flood and all buildings and gardens in the city near the river edge have been ruined. A number of horses, cows and other livestock drowned in the stables and byres of the city. No lives have been lost to the flooding, although one young woman was rescued from the river by a fellow servant after she was carried 700 yards by the fast flowing water.*

## August 1772
### NEW BRIDGE BUILT FOR DEAN AND CHAPTER
*The foundation stone of a new bridge belonging to the Dean and Chapter of Durham (Prebends Bridge) has been laid at Durham. The Dean and Chapter architect George Nicholson will be responsible for the construction of the new bridge which will replace the bridge destroyed by the great flood of November last year.*

## 1772
### ELVET MOOR DIVIDED
*The four hundred acre Elvet Moor near Durham has been divided up. The Dean and Chapter will reserve six pence per acre in rent and all revenue from mining.*

# GILLYGATE

The long, steeply banked street of Gilesgate is still occasionally known by its medieval name Gillygate meaning the street of St Giles. It is named after the nearby St. Giles Church, an attractive little building which claims to be the second oldest church in the City after the cathedral.

There are a number of interesting old houses in the street of Gilesgate but most picturesque are those situated by a Green near where a lane leads down to the river bank at Pelaw Wood. Called Gilesgate Green, this was originally separate from Gilesgate itself. This area is known locally as 'the duckpond' but there is no duckpond to be seen.

A little further up, Gilesgate splits into two parts called the Sunderland Road and the Sherburn Road and somewhere in the angle between the two (on a site now occupied by shops) stood a reputedly ancient site called the Maiden's Arbour, where a signalling station or beacon is said to have existed associated with either Old Durham or the nearby fort of Maiden Castle.

# BISHOP VERSUS BISHOP

St Giles Church is well situated back from the street of Gilesgate with commanding views from its graveyard of the Cathedral, Pelaw Wood, Maiden Castle and Old Durham. Built in 1112 by Bishop Ranulf Flambard the church was constructed as a chapel for a hospital dedicated to St Giles. The hospital stood close to the church but was burned down in the 1140s

The trouble which led to the burning of St Giles Hospital was caused by one of the most notorious characters in the history of the Bishopric of Durham called William Cumin, the usurper who had falsely appointed himself as the Prince Bishop of Durham with the encouragement of King David of Scotland. Cumin had taken up residence at Durham Castle where for three years he arrogantly abused his falsely claimed powers and terrorised the local people with the assistance of his band of armed retainers.

Cumin's activities did not of course go unnoticed and in March 1143 when William de St Barbara was elected as the true Bishop of Durham it was realised that Cumin would have to be removed. When the real bishop came north he was supported by a number of local barons including Roger Conyers. They all expected the usurper to stand down. Unfortunately he did not and what is more Cumin would not allow St Barbara anywhere near the castle. The real Bishop was forced to take refuge at St Giles Church for the night.

The following morning Cumin broke down the doors of St Giles Church and a pitched sword battle broke out between the supporters of the real bishop and the usurper. Terrified monks caught up in the fight prayed desperately for peace but one was nearly killed by a huge stone thrown by one of the usurper's men.

On this occasion William St Barbara was forced to accept defeat and had to leave Durham for a time until a second unsuccessful attempt was made to oust Cumin at a later date. In August 1144 William De St Barbara tried once again to evict Cumin by enlisting the help of the Earl of Northumberland's army. This time they were successful, Cumin's men fled the scene, though not before he and his men had burned down the Hospital of St Giles. Later Cumin was captured by Roger Conyers at Kirk Merrington near Spennymoor.

# AN ANCIENT HOSPITAL

The destruction of the hospital of St Giles by William Cumin resulted in the relocation of the hospital by Bishop Pudsey to a new site a little further north by the river Wear at Kepier.

*Gate of Kepier Hospital*

## February 11th 1773
### PORTCULLIS BROKEN
*The portcullis in the medieval gateway between Saddler Street and the North Bailey came crashing down today while workmen were busy enlarging the jail that occupies this building. This is believed to have been the first time the portcullis has been down for over a century. The workmen have cut the portcullis into pieces to restore communication between the Bailey and Saddler Street.*

## August 23rd 1773
### MAN EXECUTED FOR ROBBERY
*A man was executed at Durham today for the robbery of a Polish Jew near Darlington. The sentenced man Matthew Vasey had stolen ninety guineas from his victim.*

## February 1774
### WOMAN DIES AGED 104
*Eleanor Shipley died in Durham City this month aged one hundred and four.*

## March 2nd 1774
### TOWER COLLAPSES
*An outer tower of the castle wall collapsed during the night close to Saddler Street.*

## 1774
### REFORMER VISITS JAIL
*John Howard a prison reformer has visited Durham Jail and has severely criticised conditions in the prison.*

## 1776
### DURHAM CATHEDRAL IN NEED OF REPAIRS
*A number of general repairs to Durham Cathedral have been undertaken this year after a survey showed some parts of the fabric of the building to be in decay. The repairs will take several years at an expense of £2000 per year.*

## April 11th 1778
### NEW BRIDGE OPENED
*A new bridge, Prebends Bridge was opened to the public today. It has been built by the architect of the Dean and Chapter Mr George Nicholson.*

## 1780
### NEW CHARTER
*A new charter has been introduced for the Corporation of Durham by Bishop Egerton. Anomlaies concerning the election of the mayor have been removed from the new charter.*

*The Market Cross*

## 1780
### MARKET CROSS REMOVED
*The market cross in Durham market place has been taken down due to its ruinous condition. Part of this pillared cross will be used in the construction of a new market piazza next to St Nicholas Church.*

## July 7th 1783
### OLD SOLDIER DIES
*William Towson a former foot soldier in the Duke of Marlborough's regiment died in Durham City today aged one hundred and four.*

## 1785
### THEATRE CLOSES
*Durham's Drury Lane theatre has closed following a legal dispute regarding the lease.*

## August 1st 1785
### MAN AND WIFE EXECUTED
*William Hamilton and his wife Isabella were executed at Durham today for breaking into and robbing a house near Witton Gilbert. Two other executions also took place today of Mr Thomas Elliott for horse theft and Duncan Wright for house breaking.*

Between Gilesgate and Kepier there is another ancient building called the Chapel of St Mary Magdalene. This dates from 1451 and is now a protected ruin close to the A690 Sunderland to Durham Dual Carriageway. It lies close to a large Do-It-Yourself store and warehouse which occupies the building of the original Durham railway station of 1844. The station was the western terminus of a railway line which more or less followed the course of the present A690.

Down towards the river, the ancient Kepier Hospital remains in the form of a large vaulted gateway with rooms up above. The hospital was built to relieve the poor and to welcome pilgrims visiting Durham. It was constructed by Bishop Pudsey some time after 1153 and was presided over by a master and thirteen brethren of which six were chaplains. Records show that the chaplains were entitled to new boots twice each year while the remaining brethren were only allowed simple leather shoes.

Naturally Kepier was important for its hospitality and in 1298 King Edward I was among those entertained here. Not many years later in 1306 the 'visit' of Robert the Bruce was not so warmly welcomed. On June the 15th of that year Bruce's Scottish army swarmed towards Kepier and severely burned the building. It is likely that much of the hospital was later rebuilt as the existing gatehouse dates from the fourteenth century.

In later centuries following the Dissolution of the Monasteries, Kepier passed out of the hands of the church and in 1568 was bought by a Londoner called John Heath who was a close friend of Bernard Gilpin 'The Apostle of the North'. The Kepier Estate purchased by Heath was quite extensive and stretched as far to the east as the 'farm or grange' called Ramside now the site of a hotel well to the east of Durham.

# KEPIER QUARRY AND FRANKLAND PARK

A mile or so to the east of Kepier Hospital the River Wear forms a steep gorge which is occupied on the south bank by Kepier Wood. This wood is of great importance in the history of Durham City as it was the site of the Kepier Quarries. The remains of stone quarrying and coal drift mining can still be seen in the steep riverside escarpments occupied by pleasant woodland. Kepier's ancient quarries are significant as this was the area where most of the sandstone used in the building of Durham Cathedral was quarried many centuries ago. It is likely that the stone from Kepier was ferried upstream for the construction of the great church. Some of the stone for the cathedral also came from the area now occupied by Quarryheads Lane a little nearer to the cathedral itself.

On the northern side of the river from Kepier Wood is Frankland Wood and further west Frankland Farm. This was the site of Frankland Park, an old deer park belonging to the Bishops of Durham. Today a large part of this area is occupied by the Newton Hall Housing Estate which is one of the largest private housing estates in Europe. It takes its name from the original Newton Hall, a Georgian mansion demolished in 1926. To the north east of the housing estate is H.M.P Frankland, Durham City's second prison.

# THE ICE RINK - SITE OF THE BISHOP'S MILL

To the west of Kepier Hospital a road leads along the river bank to the large riverside green called The Sands. Since the fifteenth century this meadow has been the common pasture belonging to the freemen of the city of Durham. Across on the northern side of the river from here is Crook Hall, a building with medieval origins. Its stairway is reputedly haunted by the ghost of a Grey lady.

Back on the south side of the river, to the east of the Sands near Freemans Place is Durham Ice Rink, home of Britain's greatest ice hockey team, The Durham Wasps. The rink was founded by a very famous Durham character by the name of 'Icy Smith' and more or less occupies the site of The Bishops' Corn Mill. Here a noisy weir crosses the River Wear beneath the busy Millburngate Road Bridge.

The Bishop's mill was the place where the freemen of Durham could grind their corn. On the opposite site of the weir was the Clock Mill situated near the site now occupied by the Millburngate Shopping Centre. Mills are recorded in Durham as early as the twelfth century when they were mentioned in the Boldon Buke of 1183. The Boldon Buke was Durham's equivelant of the Domesday Book.

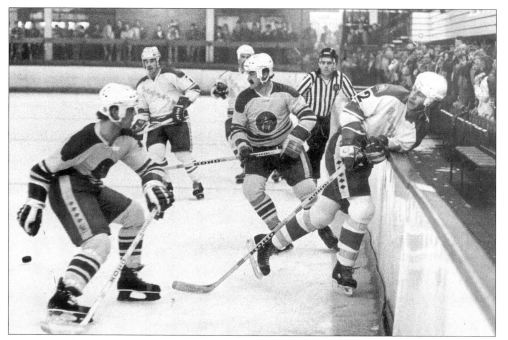

*Durham Wasps in action*

## 1790
### LIGHTING AND PAVING FOR DURHAM
*An Act has been obtained this year for paving and lighting in the city of Durham. Tolls will be imposed for this purpose.*

## 1791
### GATE REMOVED
*Clayport Gate, a medieval gateway situated at the point where Claypath joins the Market Place has been removed along with some adjoining shops and houses. The gate consisted of a weak single arch of stone and rubble with a foot passage*

## March 12th 1792
### THEATRE OPENED
*A new theatre has been opened in Saddler Street, Durham behind the Lord Nelson Inn (The Shakespeare) Opening productions will include the comedy 'Wild Oats' and the farce 'The Spoiled Child'.*

## September 17th 1793
### INFIRMARY OPENED
*A new infirmary has opened in Allergate, Durham. A procession from Palace Green to the Infirmary led by the Bishop and Dean marked the occasion. The tragedy Cato was presented at the theatre in Saddler Street to raise funds for the institution.*

## 1796
### 'DUKE' DIES IN WORKHOUSE
*Thomas French has died in the workhouse at Durham. He was also known by the assumed name 'The Duke of Baubleshire' a title for which he took great pride in pretending to be a peer of the realm. He wore a star painted on his breast, a cockade on his hat and several brass rings on his fingers. He claimed to be in regular correspondence with the king on important matters of state and defence.*

## 1798
### ARMED ASSOCIATION FORMED
*An armed association has been formed in Durham City. Five hundred inhabitants of the city enrolled, from which a band of three hundred men were selected by Ralph John Fenwick Lord Lieutenant colonel commandant.*

## July 22nd 1799
### ROPE BREAKS DURING EXE-CUTION
*Mary Nicholson was executed at Durham today for poisoning her mistress. Before the hanging was complete, the rope broke and the woman fell to the ground. The sentence was continued an hour later.*

## September 1st 1799
### DURHAM'S OLDEST WOMAN DIES
*A one hundred and two year old woman was burried at St Oswald's Church, Elvet today.*

## 1800
### SOUP KITCHEN ESTABLISHED IN DURHAM
*A soup kitchen has been established at Durham in the hall of St Nicholas Church. A great quantity of soup is to be distributed to the poor of the district who have suffered great poverty as a result of a bad harvest last year.*

## July 26th 1800
### MAN DIES AGED 102
*A man by the name of John Farrer has died in the city of Durham aged 102 years old.*

## March 14th 1801
### WOMAN LIVES TO 103
*A Mrs Eleanor Crowe aged one hundred and three died in the City of Durham today.*

## 1802
### FRAMWELLGATE MOOR DIVIDED
*Framwelgate Moor, Brasside Moor and Witton Gilbert Common (2400 acres) all near Durham City have all been enclosed this year.*

# CLAYPATH

From the Sands a road called Providence Row leads up a bank to join the ancient street of Claypath known in times past as Clay Peth meaning Clay Hill. To the east Claypath becomes Gilesgate with their boundaries marked by a vennel called Tinkler's Lane. Claypath, site of The Northern Echo's Durham office, once joined the Market Place near St Nicholas Church but was cut off by road developments in the 1960s and 70s.

In earlier times a defensive gateway stood here called the Clayport Gate, until its removal in 1791. The Clayport Gate or Clewer Port formed part of the old medieval city wall of Durham and was of importance as it controlled the movement of people in and out of the city from the east - the only part of central Durham which could be approached without crossing the river. The gate was of a 'good size' with a chamber above it. Adjoining the gate were walls which extended south towards Elvet Bridge and north along the back of St Nicholas church towards the river.

Behind St Nicholas church the city walls ran adjacent to a 16th century house called New Place or Palace which stood near the Town Hall in the Market Place. The Palace was a town house belonging to the Neville family of Raby Castle who were the most powerful barons in the County of Durham. In more recent times the locality of this palace was remembered in the name of the Palace Theatre (1909-1964), a cinema known to locals as 'The Flea Pit'. Charlie Chaplin performed here in the early days of his career, when the 'Palace' was a variety theatre.

# CARPETS AND CLOTH

From St Nicholas Church the old walls of Durham City ran south down to the River Wear where a ford once crossed to Framwellgate. Here (once again in the vicinity of the Ice Rink) a road called Walkergate passed though the wall by a small gateway called the Walkergate Postern.

Walkergate, along with Back Silver Street and a lost vennel on the north side of Claypath called Paradise Lane formed part of an ancient packhorse route.

Walkergate anciently meant the Cloth worker's street and their trade seems to have traditionally existed in this area. For a time in the early seventeenth century the old house called New Place, which had been confiscated from the Nevilles following their involvement in a rebellion against Queen Elizabeth I, was used as a woollen factory. Unfortunately the business failed, as did a second attempt to establish the trade a little later.

Eventually in 1814 a weaver from Merrington called Gilbert Henderson successfully met the challenge of establishing a business on the site and by the later nineteenth century Henderson's Durham carpets were famed throughout the world. Later the carpet factory building was bought by Mr Hugh MacKay, the Henderson's manager who started another successful Durham business. Now located at Dragonville near Gilesgate, the Hugh Mackay Factory is still producing top quality carpets.

*January 7th 1804*

**COTTON FACTORY BURNS**

At two o' clock this Sunday morning a fire began to rage at Salvin's cotton manufactory near St Oswald's Church, Elvet, Durham. Fire engines were quickly on the spot but despite the efforts of passers by who gave assistance, the fire raged and by daylight the building was reduced to a shell. The flames could be seen for miles around the city.

*1806*

**POET BORN NEAR DURHAM**

Elizabeth Barrett (later Barrett-Browning) born at Coxhoe Hall near Durham

*July 19th 1808*

**CATHOLIC COLLEGE ESTABLISHED**

Ushaw College, a Roman Catholic seminary has been established to the west of Durham City.

*1808*

**NEW BOOKSHOP**

George Andrews has established a bookshop in Saddler Street Durham.

*Jimmy Allan*

*November 13th 1810*

**GYPSY PIPER DIES IN JAIL**

Jimmy Allan known as the Gypsy piper has died while imprisoned in the House of Correction beneath Elvet Bridge.

## 1810
### NEW PRISON BUILT
*A new prison is under construction at Elvet.*

## 1811
### DEEP PIT SUNK
**Haswell near Durham**

*The sinking of a Pit at Haswell, east of Durham City has proved the existence of a coalfield beneath the Magnesian Limestone escarpment of eastern Durham. This will mark the beginning of deep mining in the east of the county.*

## June 15th 1812
### FREEMEN RIDE BOUNDARIES
*The freemen of Durham City have perambulated the boundaries of Durham City, a custom which has been neglected with the recent enclosures of the adjacent Durham moors. The procession began at ten o clock with men on horseback attended by the banners of the various trades and to the accompaniment of music and drums.*

## 1812
### NEW BUILDING FOR BLUE COAT SCHOOL
*A new building has been constructed in Claypath, Durham to house the Blue Coat School.*

## April 13th 1814
### NAPOLEON CARRIED THROUGH STREETS
*An effigy of Napoleon Bonaparte was paraded through the City of Durham to celebrate the surrender of Paris to the British allies today. The entire city has been illuminated with coloured flags and lamps to celebrate the victory and the bells of the cathedral and city churches accpompanied by musical bands have added to the great air of celebration.*

## 1814
### CARPET BUSINESS ESTABLISHED
*A weaver called Gilbert Henderson, from Kirk Merrington, County Durham has established an important carpet manufacturing business in Durham City.*

**September 10th 1814**

**ADVERTISER PUBLISHED**

*The first copy of the Durham Advertiser has been published in Durham by the firm of Francis Humble and Company. The newspaper was originally called the Newcastle Advertiser and has been removed to Durham after a change of ownership.*

**1815**

**SEARCH FOR COAL AT FRAMWELLGATE**

*Coal Boring operations have been taking place at Framwellgate near Durham City this year.*

**March 6th and 17th 1815**

**LONG LIVED RESIDENTS DIE IN SAME MONTH**

*Jane Maddison of Framwellgate, 100 years old, and Mary Paddison of Shadforth near Durham, 103 have both died this month.*

**December 29th 1815**

**WIND DESTROYS MILL**

*A paper mill belonging to a Mr Lumley of Butterby, near Durham was blown to the ground by a severe wind this night, the mill was completely destroyed. A huge quantity of paper in an unfinished state was caught up in the general ruin of the building.*

**January 3rd 1816**

**RESIDENT DIES AGED 100**

*Mrs Ann Smith of Millburngate, Durham died today aged 100 years.*

**January 13th 1817**

**MAN DIES ON HIS 100TH BIRTHDAY**

**Shincliffe**

*Mr John Lamb, a farmer died today at Shincliffe near Durham City. He was 100 years old today.*

**March 1817**

**ONE HUNDRED YEAR OLD MAN DIES IN POOR HOUSE**

*William Williamson has died in the Durham Poor House aged 100 years.*

## April 20th 1817
### 'LUNATIC' DIES

*A man known as 'Dicky the Lunatic' has died in the House of Correction at Durham City. Dicky, whose real name is thought to be Richard Williamson had been locked up in Durham for a total of 46 years and was around 80 years of age. He was first discovered in the year 1771 near the house called Newton Hall not far from Framwelgate Moor, where he was found in a complete state of nudity. It is thought that he may have escaped from some institution. The only clue to his origin was his south country accent. Dicky was completely unable to account for his origins but was able to repeat parts of a church service.*

## December 18th 1817
### 27 DIE IN PIT

*Twenty seven people have been killed in a colliery disaster at West Rainton near Durham City*

## 1817
### GILESGATE MOOR ENCLOSED

*The 270 acre moor of Gilesgate has been divided this year, it follows the enclosure of Framwellgate and Brasside Moors in recent years. The Marquess and Marchioness of Londonderry as owners of Gilesgate Moor will have one sixteenth rent as lord and lady of the manor and will reserve the mines that may be exploited in the district.*

## 1818
### KEPIER PIT FOUNDED

*A pit has been established at Kepier Grange to the east of Durham City.*

## April 14th 1819
### MAN HANGED FOR RAPE

*A 67 year old man by the name of George Atcheson has been hanged outside the new Durham County Courts for the rape of a girl under the age of ten years.*

## January 1st 1820
### DURHAM CHRONICLE PUBLISHED

*The first edition of a newspaper called the Durham Chronicle, or General Northern Advertiser has been published in the city by Mr John Ambrose Williams.*

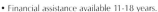
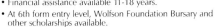

**1820**
### LAST CITY GATEWAY DESTROYED
*The Great North Gate, also known as the Jail Gate has been removed from Saddler Street. It was the last gate of Durham's historic city walls. The gate which has long been used as a prison was regarded as an obstruction to traffic.*

*Joseph Borruwlawski*

**1820**
### LITTLE COUNT ARRIVES
*The little count Joseph Borruwlawski has arrived in Durham City*

**1821**
### COURTS COMPLETE
*Durham Assize Courts have been completed by the Durham County architect Mr Ignatius Bonomi.*

**1821**
### LORD LONDONDERRY PELTED
*During a celebration of the Coronation in Durham, the Marquess of Londonderry presented a small gift of an ox for roasting at the head of Old Elvet. The ox was cut into several pieces and with small quantities of bread was thrown to the poor of the city. The city folk responded by pelting the food back at the Marquess, a man who is disliked for his uncompromising attitudes.*

**1821**
### BURN HALL BUILT
*Burn Hall has been built by the great County Durham architect Ignatius Bonomi near Croxdale, Durham.*

## 1821

### NEW PIT AT RAINTON

*The Meadows West Pit has been sunk at West Rainton near Durham. The pits in this district are the property of the Marquess of Londonderry.*

*Stephen Kemble as Falstaff*

## June 6th 1822

### GREAT ACTOR DIES

*Stephen Kemble, actor comedian and theatre owner has died at Durham City. Mr Kemble a very large man who could play Falstaff without padding, had been the manager of the Theatres Royal at Glasgow, Edinburgh and Newcastle and lately Durham. Regarded by the late playwright Richard Brinsley Sheridan as one of the best performers he had seen, Kemble had retired from acting to Durham where he had made great friends with the little count Joseph Borruwlawski. Kemble who was a published author of several ballads, addresses and songs is to be burried in the cathedral on June 11th.*

## July 11th 1823

### POET DIES

*James Brown of Old Elvet Durham known as 'The Durham Poet' died today aged 92. He had formerly been known as the Poet Laureat of Newcastle during his residence in that city.*

# DURHAM CONSTABULARY

*Aiming for Excellence*

HQ, Aykley Heads,
Durham DH1 5TT
Tel 0191 - 386 4929
Fax 0191 - 375 2160

## KEY

For general enquiries and information see map to find which of the 6 areas **you** live in

**1 WEAR & TEES**
Bishop Auckland
01388 - 603566
Crook
01388 - 762011
Barnard Castle
01833 - 37328

**2 DERWENTSIDE**
Consett
01207 - 504204
Stanley
01207 - 232144

**3 DURHAM**
Chester-le-St
0191 - 388 4311
Durham
0191 - 386 4222

**4 EASINGTON**
Peterlee
0191 - 586 2621
Seaham
0191 - 581 2255

**5 SEDGEFIELD**
Newton Aycliffe
01325 - 314401
Spennymoor
01388 - 814411

**6 DARLINGTON**
Darlington
01325 - 467681

**CRIMESTOPPERS
0800 - 555 - 111**
You need not give your name & you may be entitled to a reward

**'MINI-COM'**
Help-line for hearing impaired people
0191 - 375

# IN EMERGENCY DIAL 999 AND ASK FOR POLICE

*November 3rd 1823*
**EXPLOSION KILLS 53**
*Fifty Three people died in an explosion at Rainton Pit near Durham City today.*

*1823*
**GAS LIGHT FOR CITY**
*The City of Durham has been illuminated with gas from an aparatus erected in a field at Framwellgate. The Durham Gas Company has been founded to meet the needs of the city.*

*1824*
**DRYBURN HALL BUILT**
*Dryburn Hall, the seat of William Lloyd Wharton has been built.*

*September 27th 1825*
**FIRST PASSENGER RAILWAY**
**County Durham**
*County Durham made history today when the world's first passenger railway, The Stockton and Darlington Railway, was opened.*

*May 17th 1827*
**ST CUTHBERT'S COFFIN DISCOVERED**
**Durham Cathedral**
*During alterations to the eastern end of the cathedral the stone tomb of St Cuthbert was opened today to reveal a 1300 year old oak coffin. The coffin, found in pieces, was protected within two other wooden coffins. A complete skeleton was found swathed in vestments of linen and silk. Several cherished relics were also discovered including a small gold cross (the cross of St Cuthbert) and an ivory comb.*

*May 21st 1827*
**CATHOLIC CHAPEL**
*A new Catholic chapel dedicated to St Cuthbert has been established at Old Elvet in the City.*

*July 1828*
**TOAD FOUND IN BRIDGE BATTLEMENTS**
*During removal of old battlements from Framwellgate Bridge for repairs, a large live toad was found embedded in the stone.*

## 1828
### COLLIERY OPENS
*A new colliery has opened at Elvet in Durham City.*

## March 27th 1829
### MAN LIVES TO 103
*A Mr Robert Davison of Providence Row, Durham City died today aged 103. In this same year an Elizabeth Maughan of Durham had lived to 100.*

## May 29th 1829
### SINGING ON THE TOWER
*The old custom of singing from the cathedral tower on this date was re-established today. The choristers made their way to the top of the tower and sang three anthems.*

## May 14th 1830
### WOMAN LIVES TO 102
*Mrs Elizabeth Hodgson of South Street, Durham died today aged 102*

## August 8th 1830
### MURDER AT THE MILL
*A young girl by the name of Ann Westrop has been murdered by her friend Thomas Clarke, a servant at Hallgarth Mill near Pittington.*

## February 14th 1831
### MURDER TRIAL
*Thomas Clarke, a servant aged 19 has been sentenced to death for the murder of Ann Westrop at Hallgarth Mill near Pittington last year, he will be hanged on the 28th.*

## 1831
### NORTH ROAD BUILT
*North Road, Durham City's main Victorian throughfare has been built. Part of the road is known as King Street.*

## September 5th 1831
### ESCAPE AT ELVET PIT
*The banksman of Elvet pit nearly fell to his death in the pit shaft today after a corf of coal was accidentally lowered while he attended to it. Fortunately his feet caught on the side of the shaft as he tripped. When he was rescued and laid in a place of safety by a person who was nearby, he burst into tears when he realised how near to death he had been.*

# arket Place

## ST NICK'S CHURCH

Durham Market Place, the focal point of the city, has medieval origins but the present Market Square is largely Victorian. The most imposing features are the Guildhall, Town Hall, the church of St Nicholas and the statues of Neptune and the 3rd Marquess of Londonderry.

The spire of St Nicholas dominates the eastern side of the Market Place. It was built in 1858 by Darlington architect J.B.Pritchett and was described by the Illustrated London News of the time as 'the most beautiful specimen of church architecture in the north of England'. The Victorian church replaced an early twelfth century church of St Nicholas. Unlike the present church this building had a tower rather than a spire. In the early nineteenth century its south front was covered by a market piazza.

*The Market Place as it appeared in 1927, left; and above in 1830. The building to the left of St Nicholas Church in the picture above is New Place, or 'Bull's Head' the former palace of the Neville family. (Pictures Durham City Reference Library)*

*July 4th 1832*
### UNIVERSITY TO BE CREATED
*A Royal assent has been given for the Durham University Bill which seeks to establish a university in the city.*

*1834*
### REGATTA ESTABLISHED
*A great annual rowing regatta has been established in the city of Durham.*

*1834*
### MINING DAMAGES CHURCH
*Restoration has been carried out on the historic St Oswald's Church. Damage to the church has been caused by subsidence resulting from the nearby Elvet Colliery.*

*1835*
### MUNICIPAL ACT
*The Municipal Corporations Act has established a new structure for the government of Durham City. The Act has removed the temporal powers of the Bishop in the City of Durham.*

*1836*
### 'PRINCE BISHOP' GIVES CASTLE TO UNIVERSITY
*William van Mildert, technically the last 'Prince Bishop' of Durham, has died and the privileges and revenue of the Bishopric of Durham have passed to the Crown. Durham Castle has become part of the University of Durham on Bishop Van Mildert's request.*

*1837*
### LITTLE COUNT DIES
*The little Polish Count Joseph Borruwlawski, has died in Durham aged 98. He was 39 inches tall.*

*1837*
### CITY POPULATION IS 9,269
*The population figures for Durham City have been recorded as 9,269. The total area of the city is 330 acres.*

## 1837

### WORKHOUSE ESTABLISHED

*A new workhouse has been established in Crossgate, Durham.*

## 1838

### COAL MINING AT FRAMWELLGATE

*A Coal mine (Framwellgate Moor Old Pit) has opened in Durham.*

## 1839

### COLLEGE FOUNDED

*Bede College, a new college for the training of male teachers, has been established in Durham.*

## 1839

### KEEP RESTORED

*Durham Castle Keep, which has fallen into a ruinous condition ,has been restored. The keep will be used by Durham University.*

*Shincliffe Station building in 1986. Now a restaurant.*

## 1839

### RAILWAY STATION IS OUT OF TOWN

*A railway station has been built at Shincliffe village to the south of Durham. At present there is no station in the city itself.*

## 1840

### OBSERVATORY BUILT

*Durham University Observatory has been built*

# KING NEPTUNE

The bare-bottomed statue of Neptune was originally placed in the Market Square in 1729 to cover an octagonal pant which provided water for the people in the Market Place. Water for the pant was supplied by pipe from the Fram Well near Crook Hall across the river to the north east. Neptune, God of the sea, symbolised an ambitious plan to turn Durham into an inland sea port by altering the course of the River Wear. In 1720 the plan was to construct a canal north to join the Team, a Tyne tributary near Gateshead. Thank goodness the plan never got beyond the drawing board for it would have resulted in the joining of the Tyne and Wear. This was not what nature had intended.

In 1759 another plan was made to bring ships to Durham by making the river navigable from Durham to Sunderland. This would have needed considerable alterations to the river course, but fortunately the increasing size of ships made the plan impractical so no work was carried out. Today the only vestige of Durham as a potential sea port is the statue of good old King Neptune who has only recently returned to his Market place site.

In 1923 the pant on which Neptune stood was demolished and he was removed to Wharton Park. The poor chap was left somewhat neglected for many years until he was struck by lightning in 1978. He returned to the Market Place in 1991, sixty eight years after his original departure.

# A MAN ON A HORSE

Neptune's equestrian neighbour in full view of the Town Hall and church is the electroplated-copper statue of the third Marquess of Londonderry. Unveiled on December 2nd 1861, it depicts the Marquess on horseback in grand hussar uniform. The 3rd Marquess owned collieries in the vicinity of Durham but is principally famous as the builder of the Durham coal port of Seaham Harbour which he founded in 1828 as a rival to Sunderland. The Marquess of Londonderry's full name was Charles William Vane Stewart.

The sculptor of Londonderry's statue was Signor Raphael Monti (1818-1881) who did not, as is often thought commit suicide following the discovery of a flaw in his creation by a blind beggar man. Legend has it that Monti boasted that no one could find fault with his statue until one day a blind man pointed out that the horse had no tongue by feeling inside its mouth. The legend is, of course, a legend.

# THE TOWN HALL AND THE POLISH DWARF

Durham Town Hall is modelled on a medieval hall with hammerbeam roofing but is mainly of Victorian origin (1851). The interior of the adjoining Guildhall dates partly from the seventeenth century.

The Town Hall contains a case displaying some items of clothing and a violin which belonged to the Polish born Count called Joseph Borruwlawksi who was remarkable for many reasons including the fact that his height from head to toe was only three feet and three inches.

Borruwlawski travelled widely throughout Europe in his early life. His ready wit, gift of mimicry and musical talents always attracted him friends and admirers including the young Marie Antionette who gave him a diamond ring while he entertained the court of the Austrian empire in Vienna. Borruwlawski made a number of visits to England and gained a particular affection for Durham which he called his 'quiet place'.

*Poland was my cradle, England is my nest,*
*Durham is my quiet place where my weary bones will rest.*

In 1790 Borruwlawski finally retired at Durham where he quickly became one of the most notable members of society making friends with a famous Shakesperian actor by the name of Stephen Kemble who was a resident of Durham. Kemble was a very big man who needed no padding when he played the part of Falstaff. In company Borruwlawski and Kemble must have been something of a local curiosity.

Count Borruwlawski died in Durham on the 5th September 1837 at the grand old age of ninety seven. For his fame he was granted burial in the cathedral where his grave is simply marked 'J.B'. Find it if you can.

# SADDLER STREET, FLESHERGATE & SOUTER PETH

Saddler Street, known historically as Saddler Gate, joins the Market Place from the south and is the main route for tourists heading for the cathedral. The lower part of the street which joins the market place was originally called Fleshergate or Flesh-Hewer-Rawe. This was the street that contained the Butcher's shambles as Flesh Hewer was an old name for a Butcher. In days gone by the Flesh Hewers slaughtered their cattle in this narrow street - a very unhealthy practice indeed.

Saddler Street does not really begin until a little further up where it splits into two either side of the Magdalen Steps. Up to this point the street should really be called Fleshergate. Saddler Street is in fact the street on the right hand side of the steps, while the street to the left leading to Elvet Bridge was known historically as Souter Peth. A Souter was a shoemaker, so this street was shoemaker's peth or inclined street.

## 1840
### PIT SUNK AT FRANKLAND
*A Pit has been sunk at Frankland Park near Durham.*

## 1841
### GROCERS ESTABLISHED
*James Fowler and Son have established a Grocers Shop in Claypath, Durham.*

## 1841
### NEW PIT AT HOUGHALL
*A new pit has opened at Houghall to the south of Durham City Centre*

## 1842
### COAL SEARCH AT GRANGE
*Coal borings are being carried out on the Grange Estate near Durham*

## 1844
### SCHOOL MOVES
*Durham School has moved from Palace Green to a new site at Quarryheads Lane.*

## September 28th 1844
### PIT KILLS 95
*95 Miners have been killed in an accident at Haswell Pit east of Durham City.*

*Gilesgate Station in 1995. Now a DIY store*

## 1844
### NEW STATION OPENS
*Durham City's railway station has opened in Station Lane Gilesgate. It was designed by the railway architect T.E.Harrison.*

## 1844
### BELMONT VIADUCT OPENS
*The huge Belmont railway Viaduct has been opened linking Brasside with Belmont across the steep gorge of the River Wear in Kepier Woods.*

## 1844
### GROCER SUPPORTS MINERS
*James Fowler, a Claypath Grocer has been supplying provisons for the coal miners of Durham during their strike.*

## 1846
### HATFIELD HALL OPENS
*Hatfield College, a Hall for poorer students has been established as part of Durham University. The building stands on the site of the old Red Lion coaching Inn.*

## 1848
### OLD DURHAM PITS SUNK
*Pits have been sunk at Old Durham Colliery near Shincliffe Mill to the south east of the city. The land belongs to the Marquess of Londondery.*

## 1849
### DUCKPOND TO BE FILLED
*A report has advised that the Duckpond at Gilesgate Green be filled in the interests of public health.*

## 1851
### NEW TOWN HALL
*Durham's new Town Hall and Guildhall have been constructed in the market place by the architect P.C.Hardwick. New indoor markets have also opened behind the Town Hall.*

*Saddler Street in 1960*

## MRS MUSTARD

In the eighteenth century the western side of Saddler Street near the entrance to Saddlers Yard was the site of a factory which produced the famous Durham Mustard which was highly esteemed thoughout the country for its pungency.

> *The city of Durham is*
> *famous for seven things*
> *Wood, Water and*
> *Pleasant Walks,*
> *Law and Gospel,*
> *Old Maids and Mustard.*
> *Anon.*

The strength and taste of Durham Mustard was far superior to any mustard that had been produced before and this was all due to a discovery by an old Durham woman of the name Mrs Clements. In 1720 Mrs Clements discovered a method for extracting the full flavour from mustard seed by grinding the seed in a mill and subjecting it to similar processes used in the making of flour from wheat.

Mrs Clement's mustard gained huge popularity throughout the country and after obtaining a patent from King George I she travelled to all the great towns of England to collect orders for her product, visiting London twice a year. Later Mrs Clement's mustard business passed into the hands of a Durham stationer called Ainsley but by this time Durham Mustard faced increasing competion from cheaper brands like condiments imported from Germany.

Despite the foreign competition two other firms were producing mustard in Durham, J Balmborough in Silver Street and Simpson and Willan of Station Lane, Gilesgate. Mustard is no longer produced in Durham today and the production of the original Durham mustard has passed into the hands of Colmans of Norwich.

# SILVER STREET AND SMITHGATE

The western side of Durham Market Place is joined by Silver Street which is one of the busiest shopping streets in the town. Today it is dominated by modern shop fronts but its narrowness is a reminder of its medieval origins.

Silver Street is said to acquire its name from being the one time site of a mint where unique Durham coins were produced in the days of the Prince Bishops although a mint is known to have existed on Palace Green. Originally it may not all have been called Silver Street however as the part of the street which joins Framwellgate Bridge is thought to have been originally called Smith Gate, a street occupied by blacksmiths.

# JOHN DUCK OF DURHAM

Silver Street was once home to one of the wealthiest citizens of Durham called John Duck , whose house was demolished in 1963. His story closely resembles that of Dick Whittington.

John Duck's early life remains a mystery but he is known to have arrived in Durham in 1655 with the intention of becoming a butcher's apprentice. He approached every butcher in Durham but was refused work because he had no details of his place of birth. The concern seemed to be that he may be a Scot, and the employment of such was forbidden by the Butcher's Guild. When one butcher finally took Duck on, the Butcher's Guild persuaded him to change his mind.

Legend states that the dejected Mr Duck in a state of misery was wandering by the river side in Durham pondering over his failure to gain an apprenticeship when a passing raven dropped a coin of gold at his feet. Surtees the Durham historian tells us that this coin was 'to be the mother of a dozen more' as with this gold coin John Duck went on to make his fortune, through how exactly is not altogether clear.

Evidence suggests that Duck was not always law abiding in the way he accumulated his wealth. He is known for example to have bought cattle from a livestock thief but we do not know enough to pass judgement on him as being corrupt. By whatever means he made his fortune Mr Duck went on to become one of the wealthiest men in Durham, owning both land and collieries in the area. In 1680 he became the Mayor of Durham and ultimately progressed to the rank of a baronet when he became Sir John Duck of Haswell on the Hill.

## 1855
### BATHS BRIDGE BUILT
*A wooden footbridge has been constructed across the River Wear linking Gilesgate with the newly opened public swimming baths in Elvet*

## 1857
### RAILWAY STATION AND VIADUCT OPENED
*Durham's new railway station has opened, just to the north of the city centre. It replaces the original Durham Railway Station at Gilesgate. The railway line and station tower above the city giving outstanding views, especially from the newly opened railway viaduct, designed by the North Eastern Railway architect T.E.Harrison. Gilesgate Railway Station will be restricted to goods only.*

## 1858
### ST NICK'S REBUILT
*St Nicholas church in Durham market place has been rebuilt by Darlington architect J.B.Pritchett. It replaces the earlier medieval church of St Nicholas (1133) which was demolished last year. The church has been highly praised by the Illustrated London News for the quality of its architecture,*

## 1858
### COLLEGE FOUNDED
*The College of St Hild, a new college for the training of female teachers, has been established.*

## 1859
### MARCHIONESS TAKES OVER FRAMWELLGATE PIT
*The Marchioness of Londonderry has taken over the management of Framwellgate Old Pit at Durham City.*

## December 2nd 1861
### HORSE STATUE UNVEILED
*A statue of the Marquess of Londonderry on horseback has been unveiled in Durham City. A huge crowd and a large military presence turned out for its unveiling.*

## 1863

### BOXING CHAMPION DIES

*John Gully, a one time champion pugilist of has died in Durham City aged eighty. Gully, who once went fifty nine rounds with 'the Game Chicken' Pearce leaves behind twenty four children.*

## 1863

### NEW PANT ERECTED

*A new pant with a statue of King Neptune on top has been erected in Durham Market Place.*

## 1864

### ST GODRIC'S CHURCH BUILT

*St Godric's Catholic Church has been built.*

## 1869

### THEATRE BURNS

*A ferocious fire has completely destroyed Durham's Theatre Royal in Saddler Street.*

## November 20th 1869

### UNION FOUNDED

*Durham Miners' Association was established at a meeting of mining leaders at the Market Hotel.*

## January 1st 1870

### THE FIRST NORTHERN ECHO

*The first edition of a new newspaper The Northern Echo was published today in Darlington*

## September 24th 1870

### MILL BURNS

*The riverside mill at Kepier Hospital has burned down. The disaster should have been prevented by the mill owner's son who had fallen asleep.*

## August 12th 1871

### FIST MINERS' GALA

*The first Durham Miner's Gala was held in the city at Wharton Park.*

## 1871

### DURHAM ACQUIRES COLLEGE

*Newcastle's college of Science has become part of Durham University.*

# Framwellgate to Neville's Cross

## FLAMBARD'S BRIDGE

Framwellgate Bridge links Silver Street to the 'Old Borough' of Framwellgate on the western side of the river and was known for many years as 'Old Bridge' as it was built more than forty years before Elvet Bridge. Originally the Silver Street end of the bridge was surmounted with a tower containing a gateway. The bridge was erected in 1120 on the orders of Bishop Ranulf Flambard (1099-1128) who was appointed as Prince Bishop of Durham following a very succesful period as a minister to King William Rufus.

Over the years Flambard's bridge witnessed many notable events in Durham's history such as the murder in 1318 of the Bishop's steward Richard Fitzmarmaduke by his cousin Robert Neville 'the Peacock of the North'. The murder took place on the bridge itself and was the final result of a long standing quarrel between these two wealthy men.

Until the 1970s nearly all the city centre traffic including buses and lorries had to pass through the narrow Silver Street and over Framwellgate Bridge to get from one part of the town

*Framwellgate Bridge in 1988*

to the other. This was a terrible inconvenience to pedestrians and eventually led to the construction of the nearby Millburngate Bridge. All except occasional service vehicles are now banned from Framwellgate Bridge. The peculiar little manned police box with its closed circuit television that controlled the city traffic from the Market Place has now long since gone.

# NORTH ROAD

At the western end of Framwellgate Bridge we enter the Victorian street of 1831 called North Road. Formerly known as King Street, its most prominent building is the cinema, which was built originally as the Durham Miners' Hall. Another building of interest is the Bethel Chapel of 1861 built by the colliery owner Joseph Love who was perceived as an enemy of the Durham Miners' movement.

Today North Road is split into two sections by a roundabout, beyond which we leave the shopping area and head north towards the County Hall. There are two buildings worth noting along this section of North Road. One is a battlemented building called the Grey Tower, which is reputedly a haunted house. Occasionally a ghostly face is said to appear at the attic window but the legend is thought to arise from the 1880s when the tower was the setting for a story called 'The Waif of the Wear'.

The other building of interest in this area is St Leonard's Roman Catholic School of which part was formerly Springwell Hall, the nineteenth century residence of the afforementioned Joseph Love. Also nearby is the obelisk of 1840, a marker point for Durham University's Observatory which lies a mile to the south near Durham School.

# MILLBURNGATE AND FRAMWELLGATE

North Road superceeded the older neighbouring streets of Millburngate and Framwellgate as the main road through the western part of the city. Millburngate was the road or gate near the Mill Burn, a stream which now flows in a culvert beneath North Road to join the River Wear via an outlet pipe. Framwellgate takes its name from an old well a little further to the north and it has been suggested that Framwellgate means 'gate from well'. The Fram Well was in fact situated in Sidegate near Crook Hall and supplied water for the pant in Durham Market Place. The Fram Well superstructure is now situated alongside the A691 'Fram-wellgate Peth' where it was placed in 1959

The old streets of Millburngate and Framwellgate which formed the district of Durham called the 'Old Borough' were destoyed in the 1930s because of their poor condition and their residents were removed to a new estate at Sherburn Road near Gilesgate.

Millburngate and Framwellgate Streets included some very historic buildings which had belonged to wealthy traders but the traders gradually moved out and over the years the two streets developed into slums. Sadly most of the historic buildings were beyond preservation.

Only one building survives from the old street called Millburngate. It is a much restored fourteenth century building, timber framed above with a fifteenth to sixteenth century rear wing. It lies just inside the entrance to the modern Millburngate Shopping Centre but was originally 129 Millburngate. In 1995 building is occupied by Durham Pine.

## 1872
**FOWLER IS MAYOR**
*Durham shop owner James Fowler has become Mayor of the City. Mr Fowler was a strong supporter of Durham miners during the 1844 strike*

## March 24th 1873
**MARY ANN COTTON EXECUTED**
*The East Rainton born multi-murderess Mary Ann Cotton was executed in Durham Jail today for poisoning her son Charles Edward Cotton at West Auckland, County of Durham. She is thought to have been responsible for the deaths of 21 people including her mother, her three husbands, one lover and a number of children including her own. Mrs Cotton has been able to claim insurances from the deaths of her relatives.*

## June 15th 1873
**FIRST GALA ON RACECOURSE**
*The first Durham Miners Gala on the Durham Racecourse took place today, speakers included Alex Macdonald of Glasgow and Thomas Burt of Newcastle.*

## 1874
**COLLIERY OPENS**
**Bearpark**
*A colliery has been sunk at Bearpark to the west of Durham City. There has been mining in this area since 1456*

## June 3rd 1876
**MINERS' HALL OPENS**
*The Durham Miners' Hall has opened in North Road, Durham City.*

## April 14th 1873
**80,000 ATTEND RACES**
*A huge crowd of 80,000 people attended a race meeting in Durham City.*

## July 3rd 1875
**RAILWAY STOPS GALA TRAINS**
*The LNER Railway Company has withdrawn all trains from Bishop Auckland, Lanchester and Newcastle to Durham today because, it claims, it cannot cope with the huge number of passengers travelling to the miners' gala.*

# SITE OF THE GALLOWS

The upper section of Framwellgate Street was called Framwellgate Peth and is now the site of a modern road leading towards County Hall, Aykley Heads and Dryburn Hospital. The older part of the hospital is Dryburn House (or Dryburn Hall), the Victorian residence of William Lloyd Wharton, chairman of the North Eastern Railway Company. It was later a residence of Colonel Cuthbert Vaux, head of Vaux breweries. Dryburn served as an emergency hospital for servicemen during World War Two when its patients included German prisoners.

In earlier times the grounds of Dryburn were the site of the Durham City gallows. Here people were hanged by the neck for crimes such as murder, horse stealing, house breaking, roberry, treason and even witchcraft!. Justice could be very rough in days gone by and on one occasion during the reign of Queen Elizabeth five traders were hanged at Dryburn on suspicion that they might be gypsies. Their names were Fenwick, Arrington, Featherstone, Lancaster and Simson.

On an earlier occasion someone was hanged in this area for being a Jesuit priest and there is a legend that after his death a local stream or burn mysteriously dried up never to flow again. Hence the name Dryburn. An alternative suggestion for the name Dryburn is that it is a corruption of Tyburn, the place where criminals were hanged in London.

# THE TRAVELLING GHOST OF CROSSGATE PETH

Near Framwellgate Bridge, North Road is joined by South Street and Crossgate which continues up bank to the west, passing the historic church of St Margaret of Antioch. Further up bank the street becomes Crossgate Peth, the road leading to the site of the Battle of Neville's Cross. In days gone by when carriages, horses and carts made their journey up Crossgate Peth they would often stop for a drink along the way.

Occasionally during their periods of rest, the drivers would become aware of a peculiar, inexplicable fall in temperature. As they continued up the bank they would notice the presence of a grey, sombre looking young woman, a 'grey lady' with a newly born child in her arms. She would remain sad and silent in the cart or carriage for the course of the journey and then upon reaching Neville's Cross at the top of the bank she would mysteriously disappear.

Legend suggests that the grey lady is the ghost of a young woman who lost her husband at the Battle of Neville's Cross in the year 1346. It is said that her husband had gone to fight in the battle without receiving her farewell, as she was firmly set against him enlisting for this fight. Perhaps her ghostly journeys were undertaken in the hope of finding his body on that ages old battlefield near the top of Crossgate Peth.

In modern times, with the fall in use of horse drawn vehicles, sightings of this ghost were less frequent although some people have claimed to see the ghost of a young woman walking in this area without a child. This is thought (by those who believe in such things) to be the ghost of another girl who in Victorian times was murdered and thrown down the steps of a workhouse in the vicinity of nearby Allergate. Her assailant was a visiting soldier who confessed to the murder many years later while living abroad.

Not far from Allergate in the nearby street of Hawthorn Terrace is the firm of Harrison and Harrison the organ builders who are one of Durham City's best known industries.

# THE BATTLE OF REDHILLS OR NEVILLE'S CROSS

In 1346 the greater part of the English army of Edward III were away at war fighting against the French with the assistance of among others Thomas Hatfield, the Bishop of Durham who took along his own private army. The French were desperate for the English to be diverted and called upon King David II of Scotland to attack the English northern border. King David gladly obliged and sallied forth into England with 20,000 men who wrecked and plundered parts of Cumberland and Northumberland before entering Durham where they made camp at Bearpark to the west of the city

The Scots were comprised of three factions under the respective commands of King David, the Earl of Moray and Sir William Douglas. On the 17th October the men of Sir William Douglas went on a rampage throughout Durham straying as far south as Ferryhill where to their surprise they encountered part of an English army of some 15,000 which pursued them north.

Under the leadership of Sir Ralph Neville and supported by the men of Thomas Rokeby and Lord Percy, the English were successful in this initial encounter and a number of Scots lost their lives. Moving north the real battle took place on the Red Hills in the vicinity of a stone cross called Neville's Cross (which existed before the battle). Arrows were fired, axes hacked, swords were thrusted and as the bloodbath continued it was clear the Scots were going to lose. David, the Scottish king fled from the scene.

In the far distance praying monks spectated from the Cathedral's central tower while nearby on a hill called the Maiden's Bower at Crossgate Moor other monks watched at closer quarters. Here they held high the holy cloth of St Cuthbert, which was a call for the support of God in this battle. The call seemed on this occasion to be answered as the Scots were easily defeated.

Meanwhile in the vicinity of Aldin Grange where the road from Crossgate to Bearpark crosses a tributary of the Wear called the River Browney, a Northumbrian soldier by the name of Copeland came across a rather exciting discovery, for there beneath the arch of Aldin Grange Bridge lay hiding none other than David King of the Scots who was badly injured from two spears that had pierced his body. Copeland quickly captured the Scottish monarch and for a time the English held on to him for ransom. Eventually a fee was agreed for the return of King David to Scotland and he was released. The canny Scots never paid the fee!. The Victory at Neville's Cross was long commemorated in Durham City folklore by local children. Boys of the city traditionally claimed that if you walked nine times around the Neville's Cross and then put your head to the ground you could hear the sound of battle and the clash of arms. Unfortunately this can no longer be tried as the cross is now protected by a fence.

*The stump of Neville's Cross*

*1893*

**ELVET STATION OPENS**
*Shincliffe Station, the first railway station in the Durham City area, has closed and a new railway station has been opened in Durham City at Elvet*

*1894*

**WATER BUSINESS**
*Mineral Water Manufacturers Wood and Watsons have set up in business on Gilesgate Bank.*

*The Old Shire Hall in 1995*

*1895*

**RED BRICK HALL FOR COUNTY COUNCIL**
*A bright red brick Shire Hall has been constructed in Old Elvet as the county council's headquarters.*

*1895*

**SKATING ON THE RIVER**
*A deep layer of Ice has covered the River Wear for several weeks now. The severe winter weather has enabled the residents of the city to indulge in the pastime of skating on the river.*

*April 13th 1896*

**PIT KILLS 20**
**Brancepeth**

*Twenty people have been killed at the Brancepeth 'A' pit near Durham City*

*1896*

**FIRST WOMEN AT UNIVERSITY**
*The first four women were admitted to Durham University this year.*

# Surrounding Places

## SACRISTON, WITTON GILBERT AND PITY ME

Durham's surrounding villages are in the main former mining settlements but many have ancient origins and often have unexpected connections with Durham's ecclesiastical history.

Sacriston to the north of Durham, for example, takes its name from nearby Sacriston Heugh which means the hill of the Sacristan. In medieval times this was part of an estate which belonged to the Sacristan of Durham Cathedral Monastery. The Sacristan, also known as a Segersten or Sexton, was the man responsible for ensuring that all cleaning, repairs of windows, bells and plumbing were carried out at the cathedral. Unfortunately, the remnants of the country manor belonging to the sacristan were demolished in 1955.

To the south of Sacriston is the village of Witton Gilbert, pronounced with a soft 'G' because it is named after a Norman-French gentleman called Gilbert de la Ley. This is one of a number of villages in the Durham area which partly owe their name origins to the Norman French language. Others include Pity Me which derives from 'Petit Mere' meaning 'a Small Lake', and Bearpark which, like Sacriston, has an old connection with Durham cathedral

## BEARPARK AND USHAW MOOR

Situated between the valleys of the River Deerness and River Browney the name Bearpark conjures up the image of an old park containing bears but the name is in fact a corruption of the original Norman-French name Beau Repaire meaning 'Beautiful Retreat'. This was the site of an important country residence belonging to the priors of Durham Cathedral and encompassed an estate of 300 acres. The prior's manor house here was largely destroyed by the Scots who invaded the area in 1640 during the Civil war.

A little to the west of Bear Park is the famous Roman Catholic seminary of Ushaw College which is the main centre in the north of England for the training of Roman Catholic priests. Its establishment dates back to the foundation of the great seminary at Douai in France which was founded in 1568 to supply catholic missionaries to England during a period of catholic repression. Douai pupils included a certain John Bost who was captured in the Deerness Valley near Durham in 1594. He was executed at Dryburn on the 24th July of that year.

*Ushaw College Chapel in 1958*

In 1793, during the French revolution, the college of Douai was seized and the occupants fled to England where they were permitted to establish a college at Tudhoe near Spennymoor, moving later to Crook Hall (near Lanchester) and later Pontop Hall. In 1808 the college was finally established at its present site to the west of Bearpark.

Ushaw College is the home to a number of important historical possesions including the finger ring of St Cuthbert which may be worn by the Roman Catholic Bishop of Hexham and Newcastle on special occasions. The college is also famous for a unique brand of squash originally played at the college of Douai.

The former mining village of Ushaw Moor lies to the south of Ushaw College in the Deerness Valley. Its name means 'the wolf's wood moor' while the name of Esh Winning village a little to the west derives from the nearby smaller village of Esh meaning Ash (as in Ash Tree). The 'Winning' in Esh Winning describes the finding or winning of coal here many years ago

The history of the Deerness valley goes back a long way as a Roman road called Dere Street passed through this area. It crossed the River Deerness somewhere between Ushaw Moor and Esh on its way towards the Roman fort at Lanchester, or Longovicium as it was known in Roman times.

# BRANCEPETH CASTLE'S FAMOUS FOLK

Of all the villages that suround Durham City old Brancepeth, to the south west, is particularly well steeped in legend and history. Most of the history revolves around the adjacent Brancepeth Castle which, in spite of modern restorations, has a long story to tell.

The castle was founded many centuries ago by the chief of the Anglo Saxon Bulmer family whose last male heir, Bertram Bulmer had a daughter called Emma who married Gilbert De Neuville, a Norman baron who came to England with William the Conqueror. De Neuville's descendants were called the Nevilles and were the owners of Brancepeth Castle until the sixteenth century.

In 1569 Brancepeth was confiscated from the Nevilles by the crown following their involvement in a plot to overthrow Queen Elizabeth I called 'The Rising of the North'. The Nevilles had been the chief instigators of this rising which had been plotted at Brancepeth and Raby Castle with the assistance of the Percys who were the most powerful family in Northumberland.

## 1903
### ANCIENT WELL FOUND
*An ancient well has been discovered in the north west corner of Durham Castle courtyard.*

## 1904
### ELVET PIT CLOSES
*The Elvet Pit in Durham City has been abandoned, it once served the industries of the city.*

## July 1904
### MURDER AT MARBLE FACTORY
*Councillor Charles Lowes, owner of Lowes' Marble works, Gilesgate has been murdered by an apprentice Robert John Allen. Mr Allen, the son of a Durham prison warder has been sentenced to twenty years imprisonment.*

## 1904
### ST CHAD'S COLLEGE
*St Chad's College has been established in the City of Durham.*

## 1906
### BOWBURN PIT SUNK
**Bowburn**
*A colliery has been sunk at Bowburn near Durham.*

## 1906
### METHODIST CHURCH BUILT
*Elvet Methodists Church has been built at Old Elvet in the city. The church and the nearby Shire Hall are imposing additions to the largely Georgian street.*

## 1908
### CHURCH NOT COMPULSORY FOR STUDENTS
*Durham University has agreed that it is no longer compulsory for its students to attend church on a Sunday.*

## 1909
### ST JOHN'S COLLEGE
*St John's College has been established in the South Bailey, Durham.*

Brancepeth Castle remained in the hands of the crown for a number of years until King James I gave it to Robert Carr, Earl of Somerset. Later the castle was taken from Carr when he was found guilty of the murder of Sir Thomas Ovebury. From Carr it passed to the wealthy son of a Gateshead blacksmith called Ralph Cole who also bought Kepier Hospital.

## BOBBY SHAFTO

One very famous owner of Brancepeth Castle was Sir Henry Bellaysyse, whose daughter Mary fell in love with Bobby Shafto who lived at Whitworth Hall near Spennymoor just across the River Wear from Brancepeth. Mr Shafto was a County Durham MP elected in 1761. Mary's love for Shafto became the subject of a very famous north country song but alas Mr Shafto had eyes for someone else and Mary is said to have died of a broken heart.

> *Bobby Shafto's gone to sea,*
> *Silver buckles on his knee,*
> *He'll come back and marry me,*
> *Bonny Bobby Shafto*
> *Bobby Shafto's bright and fair,*
> *Combing down his yellow hair,*
> *He's my ain for ever mair,*
> *Bonny Bobby Shafto.*

In 1796 Brancepeth was bought by William Russell, a Sunderland banker. The Russells of Brancepeth became one of four great coal owning families in the north called the 'Grand Allies' and William's son Matthew became the richest commoner in England. Later, by marriage, Brancepeth became the property of Lord Boyne who is commemorated in the name of a public house a little further to the north at Langley Moor. There have been a number of other owners since that time.

## BRANCEPETH CHURCH

The surroundings of Brancepeth are quite pleasant and the ivy covered cottages which lead up to the castle are particularly attractive. The Brancepeth area caught the attention of both William Wordsworth who visited the place and featured Brancepeth in a poem and Albert Lord Tennyson who wrote 'Come into the Garden Maud' at Brancepeth.

Of particular interest in Brancepeth is the 12th century Church of St Brandon. This is a beautiful church in a beautiful setting. It is worth looking inside the church to view the remarkable high quality seventeenth century woodwork associated with Bishop John Cosin (1660-1672). Also inside the church is an attractive font of Frosterley Marble and the effigy of Robert Neville known as the 'Peacock of the North'. It was Sir Robert who murdered the Bishop of Durham's steward on Durham's Frawellgate Bridge in the fourteenth century.

*Brancepeth Village, Autumn 1959*

# THE BRAWN OF BRANCEPETH

Brancepeth is said to acquire its name from being the Brawn's Peth, an area frequented by a notorious brawn (or Wild boar) many centuries ago. The brawn roamed the marshy forests that once existed south of Durham in Saxon and Norman times and is said to have terrorised the local people. There is no doubt such beasts actually lived in the Durham area and there is another brawn legend associated with Bishop Auckland.

A young man by the name of Hodge from Ferryhill was employed in the pursuit of the Brancepeth Brawn and he took careful note of the paths that it frequently used. He then constructed a deep pit on the brawn's highway and covered it with boughs and earth. Hodge was successful in his pursuit. The brawn came tumbling along and went head first into the depths of the pit. Its nauseating screeches echoed throughout the countryside. No doubt the beast later ended up on someone's dinner plate.

It has been suggested that the nearby village of Brandon was anciently the site of the Brawn's lair or den but this may also be claimed by an ancient iron age site to the north west of Brancepeth called the Brawn's Den.

## 1915

### NEW PARK FOR DURHAM

*The daughter of William Lloyd Wharton of Aykley Heads has given part of her father's estate to the people of Durham as a public park called Wharton Park.*

## October 23rd 1915

### MINERS' HALL OPENS

*A new Durham Miner's Hall has opened at Redhills in the north west of the city. The building replaces the Old Miner's Hall in North Road.*

## 1918

### MARQUESS SELLS OLD DURHAM

*The Marquess of Londonderry has sold his land at Old Durham near the City to the Hopps family for the purpose of farming.*

## 1918

### BOW AND LESS MERGE

*The parishes of the churches of St Mary le Bow and St Mary the Less in the Bailey, Durham City have merged into one.*

## November 11th 11a.m 1918

### ARMISTICE DECLARED

*At the eleventh hour of the eleventh day of the eleventh month fighting ceased in the Great War. A declaration of peace was read out by George Henderson Proctor, the Mayor of Durham, from the balcony of the Guildhall in the Market Place.*

## 1919

### ST MARY'S COLLEGE

*St Mary's College has been established.*

## 1920

### NEW BISHOP

*Herbert Hensley Henson has been appointed the new Bishop of Durham.*

## April 1st 1921

### POLICE FORCES MERGE

*The City Police force consisting of a chief constable, 1 inspector, 4 sergants, and 18 constables has amalgamated with the County Police force.*

## September 1921
### COLLEGE OPENS
*Nevilles Cross College has opened.*

*Brancepeth Castle*

## 1922
### CASTLE IS INFANTRY HQ
**Brancepeth**

*Brancepeth Castle, the former home of Viscount Boyne, has become the headquarters of the Durham Light Infantry.*

## 1923
### NEPTUNE MOVED FOR TRAFFIC
*The statue of King Neptune has been removed from Durham Market Place to make way for the busy traffic which is choking the city centre.*

## 1923
### MINING REACHES PEAK
**County Durham**

*Coal mining has reached a peak in County Durham. It now employs around 170,000 miners.*

## 1923
### SCIENCE BUILDING OPENS
*A new science building for Durham University has opened to the south of the city.*

## 1924
### GOLF COURSE OPENS
**Brancepeth**

*Brancepeth Golf Course has been opened. The course was planned by Lord Boyne.*

Brandon, to the north of Brancepeth, was the colliery village chosen as the setting for Frederick Grice's delightful children's novel entitled 'The Bonnie Pit Laddie' which told of growing up in the old Durham coalfield .

# CROXDALE AND SHINCLIFFE

From Brandon a B-road leads a little way south to the junction with the Great North Road near to the point where the River Browney joins the River Wear at Croxdale. There are two great halls in this area to the east and west of the River Wear. One is Croxdale Hall which has been the seat of the Salvin family since the fifteenth century. The other is Burn Hall which was built to the designs of the Durham architect Ignatius Bonomi in 1821. It once also belonged to the Salvins but is now a Roman Catholic seminary.

To the north of Croxdale the River Wear is well wooded on its eastern side by Croxdale wood which leads north to the river crossing of Shincliffe bridge and the nearby village of Shincliffe. This village derives its name from the Anglo-Saxon 'Scinna Cliffe' meaning 'the hill of the ghost or demon' although it is a pleasant village which seems an unlikely setting for demonic activities.

In medieval times Shincliffe belonged to the priors of Durham Cathedral monastery who seemed to have got involved in several quarrels with the bishop in this area. It is recorded that in 1300 the prior was attacked by the bishop's retainers on Shincliffe Bridge and five years later the same prior complained that one of the bishop's servants had stolen a horse from him at Shincliffe and taken it off to Durham Castle. The priors park lay just to the north of Shincliffe.

# THE PITFALLS OF LOVE

High Shincliffe lies to the south of Shincliffe itself. It is now a modern estate but occupies the site of an old mining settlement called Bank Top. The pitmen who once lived here came from all parts of Northumberland and Durham but surprisingly none actually originated from Shincliffe.

The pit had been sunk around 1837 and one of its later owners was Joseph Love, a former pitman who married into wealth and became a coal owner. Despite his charitable donations to the church he had a reputation for undue harshness in his behaviour towards the miners. Love is said to have made a fortune from fining miners who, in his opinion, were not working hard enough and would also occasionally stop credit to miners at the local shops which he owned.

Love's colliery village had a population of around 3000 but in 1874 the seams had been worked and the pit was closed. Poverty quickly followed and gradually all the residents were forced to move away.

# QUARRY COUNTRY

The main road south from Shincliffe (the A177) leads to Coxhoe and may follow the course of a Roman Road. Coxhoe along with nearby Cornforth, Kelloe and Quarrington Hill are in limestone quarry country and a number of old quarries exist in the area, some protected as important nature reserves. The villages in the area are situated among the Magnesian Limestone hills which are typical of the east Durham countryside between Hartlepool and South Shields.

These limestone hills were once at the bottom of a great lagoon which was pushed to the surface by powerful earth movements in prehistoric times. The local limestone is of a type called Dolomite and contains calcium and magnesian deposits. It has been used in the past as building material most notably to cement together the stones of Durham Cathedral. Today it is in an important raw material used in the chemical industries of Teesside.

# ELIZABETH BARRETT

The village of Kelloe with a name that derives from Caluh Law (Bare Hill) had eight small coal mines in its vicinity during the last century but its history goes back well before the days of mining. Kelloe Law nearby is the site of a cist discovery dating from the Bronze Age where the skeletons of an ancient family were found, consisting of a father and mother aged about thirty and three children aged about four, eight and twelve.

A little to the east of Kelloe we are at the site of a deserted medieval village called Church Kelloe. The only remaining feature of the settlement is the Norman church of St Helen which is noted for the well preserved and beautifully detailed Norman cross dedicated to St Helena.

A tablet inside the church is also of interest, commemorating the birth of Elizabeth Barrett Browning, who was born nearby at Coxhoe Hall in 1806. Elizabeth's family provided the model for the 'Barretts of Wimpole Street'. Her birthplace was demolished in 1952.

# THE VICAR OF KELLOE

One of the Bishops of Durham, Richard De Kellaw (1311), is known to have originated from Kelloe. He was much troubled by Scottish invasions which were fought off by the forces of the bishopric under the leadership of the bishop's brother Patrick.

Another notable resident of Kelloe was John Lively the seventeenth century vicar of Kelloe who was noted for the fact that he had no male heir:

> *Here lies John Lively,*
> *Vicar of Kelloe who*
> *had seven daughters*
> *but never a fellow.*

Not far from Kelloe is Beacon Hill, the site of a Napoleonic warning beacon, and also nearby is Signing Bank where pilgrims traditionally first encountered Durham Cathedral.

An alternative name for the hill is asylum bank and was perhaps the route the criminals took to Hartlepool, on leaving the sanctuary at Durham Cathedral. A little further to the north is a pretty little valley called Cassop Vale. In early times this was a hunting area for Durham's Prince Bishops. Its name derives from Cat's Hop meaning valley of the wild cats.

## 1925
### MINERS THROW DEAN INTO BOAT
*Miners have tried to throw the Dean of Durham into the river at their gala in Durham after mistaking him for the right wing Bishop of Durham Hensley Henson. The Dean fell into a boat.*

## 1926
### NEWTON HALL DEMOLISHED
*The old Georgian House called Newton Hall to the east of Framwellgate Moor has been demolished. The building was at one time a branch of the Durham County lunatic asylum.*

## 1926
### PINEAPPLE LOSES LICENCE
*The Pineapple Inn at Old Durham has lost its licence to sell alcoholic drinks. The inn and surrounding area is a popular place for recreation and picnics.*

## 1926
### SCHOOL CHAPEL BUILT
*Durham School Chapel has been constructed in memory of Dunelmians killed in the First World War.*

## 1926
### MARKET PALACE SITE SOLD
*The Henry Smith's charity has sold the whole of the 'New Place' site on which the Town Hall and part of the covered market are built to the Durham Corporation for £4000. The New Place was the site of a palace belonging to the Neville family and was demolished in 1852*

## 1927
### POST OFFICE MOVES
*Durham Post Office has moved from Saddler Street to Claypath.*

## 1928
### NEW BUS STATION TO OPEN
*A new bus station is being built in Durham City adjacent to the city's North Road*

**1928**

**HISTORY PUBLISHED**

*The third volume of the Victoria County History of Durham has been published, covering Durham City and Stockton. The first two volumes covering natural , politcal, and socio-economic history were published in 1905 and 1907. Volume three was delayed by the war.*

**1931**

**STATION CLOSES TO PASSENGERS**

*Elvet railway station in Durham City will cease to be used for passenger services.*

**September 28th 1932**

**BATHS OPENED**

*New baths have been opened in the city by Lord Barnard*

**1934**

**COTTAGES DEMOLISHED**

*A group of sixteenth century cottages have been demolished in Framwellgate for development – despite opposition.*

**1936**

**ROMAN TILES FOUND**

*Roman tiles have been discovered by a local man in the vicinity of Old Durham, Gilesgate.*

**December 12th 1936**

**KING ABDICATES**

*King Edward VIII has abdicated from the throne because of his love for American divorcee Wallis Simpson.*

**1937**

**UNIVERSITY SPLITS**

*Reorganization of Durham University has recognised two divisions; Durham and Newcastle. The latter division of colleges are to be grouped under the title of King's College*

**May 12th 1937**

**KING GEORGE CROWNED**

**Westminster Abbey**

*King George VI has been crowned at Westminster Abbey.*

# LUDWORTH TOWER

North of Cassop the little villages of Shadforth and Ludworth have names that mean 'Shallow Ford' and 'Ludda's Farm'. Ludworth is noted for the ruins of a Pele Tower a feature very common in Northumberland but rare in County Durham. Peles are oblong tower houses built to protect local people from Scottish invasions.

The fortification at Ludworth was constructed in 1422 by the Holden family on the site of their manor. A large part of the building collapsed in 1890 but one wall remains along with the foundations of a tight spiral staircase which is a typical feature of a pele tower.

# SHERBURN AND PITTINGTON

To the north west of Shadforth is the village of Sherburn (From Scir Burn meaning 'Bright Stream') and the nearby Sherburn Hospital which was founded in 1181 by Bishop Pudsey as an asylum for lepers. Most of Pudsey's buildings were destroyed by an invasion of Scots and today the only original part of the building is the chapel.

Sherburn Hospital lies on the banks of the Old Durham Beck which joins the River Wear near Old Durham. In times gone by this stream was also known as the Sher Burn or the River

*Interior of Pittington Church which closely resembles the architecture of the Cathedral's Galilee Chapel*

Pitting. Upstream the beck leads to Pittington which is the site of the historic Norman Church of St Lawrence

Pittington church underwent some restoration by Ignatius Bonomi in the nineteenth century but it has some notable surviving medieval features in the form of the nave, the tower and the north arcade. The Norman arches and zig zag decorated pillars in the church are strikingly similar to those found in Durham Cathedral. Some of the features of the church interior are very similar to the cathedral's Galilee chapel. The reason is that both were built by Christian, the master architect of Hugh Pudsey, a twelfth century Bishop of Durham. Christian was granted land in the Pittington area by the bishop.

# THE HALLGARTH MURDER

In the nineteenth century Hallgarth near Pittington was the scene of a very famous northern murder in which a nineteen-year-old servant boy at a local mill by the name of Thomas Clarke was accused of the murder of a servant girl of the same age by the name of Ann Westropp.

It was at 6 o'clock in the evening of Sunday 14th August 1831 while the mill owners were away that Thomas Clarke, in a most distressed state, alarmed the residents of the village of Sherburn with the information that six Irishmen had broken into the house at Hallgarth. He claimed that they had ransacked the house for its money, and then assaulted him with a poker before brutally murdering the servant girl.

Returning to the mill with the people he had informed, the girl's body was found in the kitchen with several wounds including a cut to her throat from ear to ear. Upon further investigation it was found that money had been stolen from the household and that a whitewashed tool had been used to break into the drawers containing the money. It was then discovered that Clarke's room had recently been whitewashed and in that room was found a blunt piece of metal which would have fitted the identity of the tool used in the robbery.

Further suspicions that Clarke was the murderer arose when it was realised that he bore no signs of an attack upon him. Moreover Clarke and the girl had been seen together earlier in the day and he had apparently been overheard to comment on some 'saucy remark' which she had made.

Huge crowds turned out for Clarke's trial at Durham on Valentines Day, February 14th 1831, and despite Clarke's calm plea of innocence he was found guilty. On Monday 28th February he was hanged on the order of the judge. His last words were;

'Gentlemen, I am innocent. I am going to suffer for another man's crime'

The Hallgarth murder became the subject of a local ballad recalled in the Monthly Chronicle of North Country Lore and Legend 1891;

*Eighteen hundred three times ten,*
*August the eighth that day*
*Let not that Sunday and that year*
*From memory pass away*
*At Hallgarth Mill near Pittington*
*Was done a murder foul*

## 1937
### CITY POPULATION 21,268
*Durham City's population is 21,268. The total area of the city is 4,029 acres.*

## September 3rd 1939
### NATION AT WAR
*Neville Chamberlain has announced that the Nation is at war with Germany*

## 1939
### NEW BISHOP
*Alwynn Terrell Petre Williams has been appointed the new Bishop of Durham.*

## 1941
### BOMBS HIT FOUNDRY
*Four German bombs have been dropped on a disused foundry site where marine equipment was once made, at the Grange near Gilesgate, Durham City.*

## 1943
### TRUST FOUNDED
*Dean Allington, a fromer headmaster of Eton School has established the Durham City Trust.*

## 1944
### ST AIDANS FOUNDED
**Shincliffe**
*St Aidan's, a society of Durham University has been established at Shincliffe to the south of the city.*

## 1944
### SHARP PLAN FOR DURHAM
*Mr Thomas Sharp, a former executive of the Ministry of Town Planning has put forward plans for the redevelopment of Durham City's road stucture.*

## March 15th 1944
### FREEDOM OF CITY GRANTED TO DLI
*The freedom of the city of Durham has been granted to the Durham Light Infantry.*

*May 8th 1945*

**VE DAY**

*Victory in Europe was declared today.*

*June 8th 1946*

**CITY CELEBRATES VICTORY**

*Victory Day celebrations have been held in Durham today. Events for the day included hymns in the market place, boating and boat races, children's sports, a grand cricket match, dancing in the Town Hall, and a prize for the best decorated house. The cathedral and castle were floodlit form dusk to 2am.*

*February 22nd 1947*

**MINERS' MEMORIAL**

*A miners' memorial has been unveiled in Durham Cathedral in memory of miners who have lost their lives working in the pits of County Durham.*

*October 23rd 1947*

**PRINCESS VISITS**

*Princess Elizabeth, the future Queen of England, has visited Durham. During her visit she laid the foundation stone of St Mary's College and made a visit to Durham Cathedral.*

*May 23rd 1950*

**FIRST LADY MAYOR**

*Hannah Harrison Rushford has been elected as Durham's first Lady Mayor.*

*October 1951*

**FOOTBALL GROUND OPENS**

*Ferens Park, the home of Durham City Football Club was opened this month.*

*1951*

**CITY POPULATION 19,000**

*The census has shown that there has been little change in the population of Durham City in the last thirty years. The figure of 19,000 is still more or less the same as it was in 1921.*

*1952*

**JOHNSTON SCHOOL MOVES**

*The Durham Johnston School has been moved from its original site at South Street, Durham to a new building at Crossgate Moor.*

*The female weak- the murderer strong*
*No pity for her soul.*
*Her skull was broke, her throat was cut,*
*Her struggle was soon o'er;*
*And down she fell, and fetched a sigh,*
*And weltered in her gore.*
*Her fellow servant, Thomas Clarke,*
*To Sherburn slowly sped,*
*And told a tale that strangers six*
*Had done the dreadful deed.*
*Now, woe betide thee, Thomas Clarke!*
*For this thy coward lie;*
*A youth like thee for girl like her*
*Would fight till he did die.*
*'They've killed the lass,' it was his tale,*
*'and nearly have killed me'*
*But when upon him folk did look,*
*No bruises could they see.*

## BELMONT AND RAMSIDE

There are two notable old mansions in the vicinity of Pittington one of which is the eighteenth century Elemore Hall, birthplace of Ann Isabella Milbanke the wife of the poet Lord Byron. The other is a battlemented hotel called Ramside Hall, a building originally called Belmont Hall by Thomas Pemberton the coal owner who constructed it as a mansion in 1820.

Pemberton surrounded the hall with extensive plantations and the whole park acquired the name of Belmont. The building is now called Ramside from the name of an old grange or farm which stood on the site of the Hall. Today Belmont is the adopted name of a large housing estate adjacent to the former mining village of Carrville

## WEST RAINTON

To the north of Belmont is the village of West Rainton, which was once an important coal mining area where former colliery owners included John Duck, 'Durham's Dick Whittington' and the third Marquess of Londonderry who had a reputation as a very hard-hearted employer.

The spire of the Victorian church at Rainton is a very prominent feature and can be seen from miles around. It was donated to the church by local MP Sir George Eliott in 1877. A large granite tablet records the donation of the spire by the MP - this tablet being of special interest in that it is a piece of stone taken from the great pyramid of Ghizeh in Egypt. It had been removed from the pyramid with the permission of the Khedive of Egypt.

# ST GODRIC OF FINCHALE

Just over a mile to the west of West Rainton across the other side of the River Wear are the ruins of Finchale Priory which is one of the most historic sites in the district of Durham City.

Finchale is mentioned as early as A.D 792 when it was the site of a synod for the Northumbrian Church held to discuss church discipline. The meeting was followed by another two in A.D 798 and in 810, which suggests that Finchale was a place of considerable importance.

In about 1104 Finchale became the site of a hermitage belonging to Saint Godric who lived here for sixty years. Godric was born in Norfolk in the year 1065 and in his early years lived the life of a pedlar but later became a sea captain and travelled extensively throughout Europe. In the middle part of his life he went on a pilgrimage to Compostella in Spain where he made the decision to return home to England to live the life of a hermit.

For a time he established a hermitage at Carlisle before moving on to Wolsingham in Weardale where he lived in a cave. Following the death of a close friend Godric witnessed a vision in which he was instructed to go to a place called Finchale. He knew of the site and got the permission of the Bishop of Durham, Ranulf Flambard, to establish a hermitage there. Here he built a wooden hut as a simple place of residence and committed himself to a life of prayer.

During his time at Finchale, Godric is said to have been troubled by fiends and demons who took various shapes and forms, most often appearing in the form of a damsel. Visited by 'evil concupience' he would do anything to rid himself of this trouble such as rolling naked in thorns and then pouring salt into his wounds.

On other occasions Godric would stand naked in the river for a whole night with the water up to his neck, although it is said that often the devil would make a sneaky appearance at the river bank and make off with his clothes.

Godric's activities, however eccentric they may appear, do not seem to have done the saint any harm as he lived to the grand old age of one hundred and five. His burial place lies among the ruins of the Finchale priory.

# FINCHALE'S SECRET PASSAGE

Following Godric's death Finchale passed into the hands of the priors of Durham Cathedral Monastery and a Benedictine priory was built there around 1196 by Henry Pudsey son of Hugh, Bishop of Durham. From the fourteenth century the priory had four resident monks but the monks of Durham Cathedral made regular visits to Finchale which they used as a kind of holiday retreat. Visiting in groups of four, the monks took it in turns to holiday at Finchale.

It is most likely that the monks travelled to Finchale above ground but there is a legend that a secret passage runs underground from Durham Castle to Finchale. Legend has it that in the eighteenth century the passage was discovered by a blind fiddle player who walked with his dog along the passage while playing the fiddle. The sounds of the fiddle could be heard above ground and this enabled the listeners to follow his course as far as Framwelgate Bridge where the passage was said to pass underneath the River Wear.

Mysteriously, upon reaching this point, the music stopped and the fiddler was never seen or heard of again. His dog is said to have turned up later above ground, with a ghostly look upon its face, but the secret passage has never been found.

*1952*
## NEW BISHOP
Arthur Michael Ramsey has become the new Bishop of Durham.

*1952*
## OLDEST BUILDING IS BACK IN USE
The Norman Chapel at Durham Castle has been reintroduced as a place of worship. The chapel which dates from 1080 is reputedly the oldest building in Durham and had fallen out of use in the sixteenth century.

*1953*
## HORSE STATUE REMOVED
The equestrian statue of the Marquess of Londonderry has been temporarily removed from the Market Place for a few months to undergo repairs.

*May 31- June 6th 1953*
## CORONATION CELEBRATIONS
Durham City has been celebrating the Coronation of Queen Elizabeth II. Events organised include bands, special services, cricket matches, amateur drama, bowls tournaments, golf championships, a swimming gala and a special coronation regatta. Special TV broadcasts of the Coronation have taken place in various church and community halls.

*April 6th 1955*
## PM IS DURHAM FREEMAN
Anthony Eden, the new Prime Minister of Great Britain is a freeman of Durham City. Eden, born in County Durham was made an honourary freeman of the city in 1945.

*1956*
## NEW BISHOP
Maurice Henry Harland has been appointed the new Bishop of Durham.

*The Durham Light Infantry*

## 1958

### DLI CELEBRATES 200 YEARS
**Brancepeth**

*Princess Alexandra of Kent who is Colonel in chief of the Durham Light Infantry attended the bicentenial parade of the regiment at Brancepeth Castle.*

## 1959

### GREY COLLEGE OPENS
*Durham University's Grey College has been founded.*

## 1960

### NEW COUNTY HALL
*The construction of a new County Hall has started at Aykley Heads to the north of Durham City. The new buidling will be the administrative headquarters for County Durham and will replace the Old Shire Hall in Old Elvet Durham which currently serves that purpose.*

## 1961

### LIBRARY OPENS
*The new Durham County Library has opened in South Street, Durham.*

## 1961

### SAVINGS OFFICE TO MOVE NORTH
*A decision has been made to move the National Savings Office, currently based in London, to Durham City. From June the office will be based at Aykley Heads until a new site is chosen.*

## 1961

### NEW MUSEUM
*The Gulbenkian Museum of Oriental Art has been completed in Durham.*

## 1961

### ST AIDAN'S COLLEGE OPENS

*St Aidan's College based on the original St Aidans Society at Shincliffe has opened in Durham. This new university college has been designed by the architect Basil Spence.*

## 1962

### NEW BATHS BRIDGE OPENS

*A new Baths Bridge has been opened in Durham City linking Gilesgate and Elvet. The new footbridge replaces an earlier iron structure built in 1898.*

## 1963

### NEWCASTLE UNIVERSITY GOES IT ALONE

*Durham University's King's College, Newcastle has become the University of Newcastle upon Tyne and will now be independent of the University of Durham.*

## 1963

### TRAFFIC INQUIRY

*An inquiry has been made into the need for reducing traffic and improving shopping facilities in the historic city of Durham*

## 1963

### PUB DEMOLISHED

*The Tanners Arms pub in Framwellgate has been removed for redvelopment.*

## 1963

### STATION DEMOLISHED

*Elvet Railway Station has been demolished to make way for new Magistrates Courts.*

## 1963

### BRIDGE BUILT

*Ove Arup has built the Kingsgate footbridge in Durham City to link university buildings on either side of the River Wear. The concrete structure was made in two sections swung together to meet in the middle.*

## 1963

### DUCK'S HOUSE DESTROYED

*The former house of John Duck, a seventeenth century mayor of Durham, known as Durham's Dick Whittington has been demolished in Silver Street.*

## October 1963

### COUNTY HALL OPENED

*The Duke of Edinburgh has opened Durham's new County Hall at Aykley Heads in the northern environs of the city. The Old Shire Hall in Old Elvet has become the new administrative headquarters for the University of Durham*

## 1964

### PALACE THEATRE DEMOLISHED

*Durham's Palace Theatre picture house near the Market Place has been demolished to make way for new developments.*

## October 29th 1964

### SCIENCE BUILDINGS OPEN

*A new science block has been built for Durham University to the south of the city.*

## 1965

### VAN MILDERT COLLEGE FOUNDED

*Van Mildert College has opened as the latest college of the University of Durham. The college is named after William Van Mildert, the last Prince Bishop of Durham who helped to establish the Unversity in 1832.*

## 1965

### NEW MOTORWAY

*The first section of a new motorway through County Durham has been built in the south of the county bypassing the town of Darlington.*

## 1965

### CIVIC AWARD FOR BRIDGE

*The Kingsgate Bridge in Durham has received a Civic Trust Award for its architectural design.*

*Dunelm House*

### 1965
**DUNELM HOUSE OPENS**
*Durham University's Student Union Building has opened. It is a concrete building on the river bank linked to the Durham peninsula by the new Kingsgate Bridge.*

### 1965
**SAVINGS OFFICE STARTED**
*The construction of Millburngate House, the new home of the National Savings Office has commenced.*

### 1966
**DRILL HALL DEMOLISHED**
*The headquarters of the eighth Durham Light Infantry at Gilesgate has been demolished to make way for new developments.*

### 1966
**NEW BISHOP**
*Ian Thomas Ramsey has been appointed the new Bishop of Durham*

### 1966
**RAILWAY STATION CLOSES**
*Gilesgate Goods Station has closed. The building was once the main passenger railway station in Durham City.*

### 1966
**ANCIENT PARISHES MERGE**
*The combined parishes of St Mary le Bow and St Mary the Less in the Bailey, Durham have merged with the neighbouring parish of St Oswald's church in Elvet.*

*1967*

## ROAD BRIDGE OPENS

*Durham's Millburngate Road Bridge has been opened. It will help to considerably ease traffic congestion in the city. A number of new road developments are under way and the new A690 road linking Durham with Sunderland has been completed.*

*July 1967*

## COLLIERY CLOSES

**Bowburn Durham**

*Bowburn Colliery south of Durham City has closed*

*1967*

## LEATHER WORKS CLOSES

*Blagdon's Leather works in Framwelgate has closed.*

*1968*

## DLI ABOLISHED

*The Durham Light Infantry has ceased to exist after merging with three other light infantry regiments. A museum has been established in Durham City in memory of the old regiment.*

*1968*

## THE PRESERVATION ZONE

*The city centre of Durham has been designated a Conservation zone. This will severely restrict development in the city.*

*Oct 29th 1968*

## MCVICAR ESCAPES

*John McVicar has escaped from E Wing of Durham Prison. Running through the city streets and swimming across the River Wear twice, McVicar ran as far as Chester-le-Street.*

*1969*

## FIRE DESTROYS FACTORY

*Fire has destroyed some of the buildings of Hugh Mackays Factory in Durham City.*

*1970*

## NEW GARDENS

*The Botanic Gardens have been established to the south of Durham City centre.*

*Home to the Legend of the Brancepeth Boar. This wild creature roamed this land in ancient times.*
*For the past seventy years wild creatures have again been seen on this land, these however have been golfers trying to come to terms with this challenging golf course*

Designed by H. S. Holt, this spacious course in parkland surroundings is regarded by many as the premier course in the north and is a true test for all categories of golfers

**Some 6,375 yards with a strict Par and S.S.S. of 70, Brancepeth is renowned for its quality greens and fairways, its Par 3s, its ravine holes and the views from the castle and surrounding countryside**

The Clubhouse, converted from the castle stables, provides a unique setting to relax and enjoy a quiet drink and meal. This private members club welcomes all visitors, societies and parties by arrangement

Secretary: - Mr K. Stewart
Steward & Stewardess: - Mr and Mrs M. Scott
**Telephone No. (0191) 378 0075 Fax No. (0191) 378 3835**
Professional: - Mr D. C. Howdon
**Telephone No. (0191) 378 0183**
**Brancepeth Castle Golf Club Limited,**
**The Clubhouse, Brancepeth, Durham, DH7 8EA**

*March 31st 1970*
**PRINCESS OPENS OFFICES**
*Princess Alexandra has offically opened Millburngate House, the headquarters of The National Savings office.*

*1970*
**HUGH MACKAY MOVES TO DRAGONVILLE**
*Hugh Mackays, the internationally renowned carpet makers have moved from their city centre factory site to Dragonville on the eastern outskirts of the city.*

*1970*
**McVICAR CAUGHT**
*John McVicar, who escaped from Durham Prison in 1968, has been captured hiding in a flat in London*

*John McVicar*

*1970*
**CHURCH REDUNDANT**
*St Mary le Bow Church in the Bailey Durham has ceased to be an opperational church. Services have transferred to St Oswald's Church in Elvet.*

*1971*
**SHOPPING CENTRE**
*The Bovis Property Division and the Building Design partnership have successfully won a competition to build a shopping centre at Millburngate, Durham. The competition was held in consultation with the Royal Fine Arts Commission.*

*December 1971*
**ASSIZES BECOME CROWN COURTS**
*Durham Assizes Courts have become Durham Crown Courts by an Act of Parliament.*

## 1971

### WATERLOO DEMOLISHED

*The Waterloo Hotel, an historic building at the eastern end of Elvet Bridge has been demolished.*

## 1972

### COLLEGE OPENS

*Durham University's Collingwood College has opened. It is named after a famous Cambridge matthematician*

*The only building to survive Millburngate development. In 1995 this building is occupied by Durham Pine.*
*(Picture Durham City Reference Library)*

## 1973

### DEMOLITION IN MILLBURNGATE

*Some of the last remaining houses in the historic area of Durham called Millburngate have been demolished for redevelopment.*

## 1973

### HABGOOD IS BISHOP

*John Stapylton Habgood has been appointed as the new Bishop of Durham.*

## 1973

### HISTORIC SQUARE DEMOLISHED

*Durham's historic Museum Square, adjoining the Bailey has been demolished. It was once the site of the University's museum. The site is to be redeveloped for student accommodation*

*April 1st 1974*
**LOCAL GOVERNMENT REFORMS CHANGE SHAPE OF DURHAM**
*Local Government reforms have considerably changed the shape of County Durham's boundaries and the boundaries of the City of Durham have been expanded to include Brandon and Byshottles and Durham Rural District Council.*

*1975*
**NEW MULTI STOREY CAR PARK**
*A huge multi storey car park has opened in Durham, to ease the parking problems associated with the historic city. The building has been given mock battlements which are thought to emulate the ancient city walls.*

*November 18th 1975*
**TRAFFIC BOX REMOVED**
*The famous traffic contol box in Durham's Market Place, above, was removed today. The box, once occupied by a policeman had TV sets linked to cameras on Framwellgate and Elvet Bridge which monitored the flow of traffic through the Market Place. Pedestrianisation of the Market Place has removed the need for traffic control.*

*1976*
**TRAFFIC RESRICTIONS IN MARKET PLACE**
*With minor exceptions traffic has been banned from Silver Street, Elvet Bridge and Durham Market Place. This will greatly ease congestion in the City Centre and make life more pleasant for pedestrian visitors to the city.*

## 1976
### NEW BRIDGE OPENS
*New Elvet Bridge has opened to traffic in Durham, making a great improvement to the traffic flow through the city centre.*

## 1976
### HILD AND BEDE AMALGAMATE
*The colleges of St Bede and St Hild in Gilesgate, which were established respectively for the training of male and female teachers have amalgamated into one. The new college will be called the College of St Hild and St Bede.*

## 1977
### BUSINESS SCHOOL OPENS
*Durham University Business School has opened.*

## 1978
### NEPTUNE HIT BY LIGHTNING
*The statue of King Neptune in Wharton Park has been struck by lightning. A fund will be established for its repair.*

## 1978
### CHURCH BECOMES HERITAGE CENTRE
*St Mary le Bow Church in the Bailey has become Durham City's Heritage Centre - a museum dedicated to the history of the city.*

## 1978
### TREASURY OPENED
*Durham Cathedral Treasury has been opened to the public as a museum. It displays many ancient relics associated with Durham City's past.*

## 1978
### SHOPPING CENTRE AWARD
*Durham's new Millburngate Shopping Centre has won a Civic Trust award and a Europa Nostra Award for its architectural design. This success follows an award received last year from the RIBA*

## 1978
### COFFIN RESTORED
*The ancient coffin of St Cuthbert has been restored.*

*May 4th 1979*
**MRS THATCHER IS PM**
*Margaret Thatcher has been elected Britain's first woman Prime Minister.*

*1979*
**800 YEARS SINCE CHARTER**
*It is 800 years since the privileges of Durham City were first confirmed by a charter of Bishop Pudsey in 1179*

*1979*
**COLLEGES JOIN UNIVERSITY**
*The College of St Hild and St Bede has become a part of the University of Durham.*

*1980*
**INVINCIBLE ADOPTION**
*Durham City has adopted HMS Invincible.*

*1980*
**HISTORIC ZONE EXTENDED**
*The boundaries of Durham City's Conservation zone have been extended. This is a recognition of the importance of preserving historic sites and buidlings in the historic city centre.*

*1981*
**NEW STATUE FOR CATHEDRAL**
*A statue of St Cuthbert has been placed in the cloister garth of Durham Cathedral. The statue was carved by sculptor Fenwick Lawson from a famous elm tree which once stood outside the North Door of Durham Cathedral.*

*1981*
**MORE SHOPS**
*Teesland Development Company has won a competition to build the second phase of the Millburngate Shopping Centre*

*1982*
**ANNIVERSARY**
*Durham University is 150 years old this year.*

*July 16th 1983*
**100TH GALA HELD**
*The 100th Durham Miner's Gala was held today. The gala has been held every year since 1871 with the exception of the war years.*

## 1984
### WORLD'S MOST BEAUTIFUL BUILDING
*As a celebration of the 150th anniversary of the Royal Institute of British Architects, a panel of 50 architectural experts have voted Durham Cathedral the most beautiful building in the world.*

## 1984
### JENKINS IS BISHOP
*David Jenkins, left, is the new Bishop of Durham. Jenkins is noted for outspoken and controversial beliefs.*

## 1984
### FIRE DAMAGES CHURCH
*A fire has destroyed the roof and chancel of the historic church of St Oswalds, Durham. .*

## April 1984
### SHOPPING CENTRE ON STAMP
*Durham's Millburngate Shopping Centre has been commemorated on postage stamps as an outstanding example of urban renewal.*

## 1984
### POPULATION IS 88,800
*Durham City's population is 88,800 living in a total area of 46,870 acres. The population figure includes prisoners and students.*

## January 1985
### CHURCH FIRE
*The Roman Catholic Church of St Godric's in Durham City has been damaged by fire.*

## 1985
### COLLIERY CLOSURES
*Sacriston Colliery has closed. It follows the closure of Bearpark Colliery last year. These were the last two collieries in the Durham City area.*

## 1986
### NEPTUNE RESTORED
*King Neptune's statue, struck by lightning at Wharton Park in 1978, has been restored.*

**MIDLAND**

*Member* HSBC  *Group*

# Supporting the Community

## November 22nd 1986
### THEATRE OPENS
*A seventy-seat theatre known as The City Theatre has opened behind the Market Place. The theatre is a venue for amateur productions.*

## April 15th 1987
### SHOPPING CENTRE OPENING
*Phase Two of the Millburngate Shopping Centre has been officially opened.*

*Sculptor Colin Wilbourne in The Upper Room*

## 1987
### TREE CARVING
*A remarkable carving entitled 'The Upper Room' depicting the Last Supper in a cluster of tree stumps has been erected on the river banks overlooked by Durham Cathedral.*

## 1987
### WORLD HERITAGE SITE
*Durham Cathedral and Castle have been declared a World Heritage Site, one of only a few selected in this country by UNESCO. A plaque on Palace Green commemorates this important status.*

## 1989
### VIADUCT STRENGTHENED
*Durham viaduct has been cleaned, strengthened and waterproofed. Overhead masts have been erected for electrification of the main line.*

## April 1990
### UNIVERSITY'S JAPANESE LINK
*The Teikyo University of Japan at Durham has been established. Students from Japan can now study for a year alongside students of Durham University.*

## 1991

### NEPTUNE RETURNS

*The statue of King Neptune is back in Durham Market Place after many years of absence.*

## 1992

### USTINOV IS CHANCELLOR

*Actor Sir Peter Ustinov, left, has succeeded Dame Margot Fonteyn as Durham University Chancellor.*

## 1992

### FIRST CLASS DURHAM

*Durham County Cricket Club has joined the first class cricket league*

## 1993

### CATHEDRAL 900 YEARS OLD

*Durham Cathedral is celebrating its 900th year. The construction of the cathedral was commenced in the year 1093 by the Prince Bishop William St Carileph.*

## 1994

### NEW BISHOP

*Michael Turnbull is the new Bishop of Durham.*

## 1995

### ONE THOUSAND YEARS OF DURHAM CITY

*Durham is 1000 years old. It was in the late summer of 995 AD that the monks carrying the coffin of St Cuthbert established a settlement at 'Dun Holm' as the final resting place of their saint.*

*Durham City Seal presented by Matthew Pattison to the Corporation of Durham 1606*